Faith in Conservation

New Approaches to Religions and the Environment

Faith in Conservation

New Approaches to Religions and the Environment

Martin Palmer *with* Victoria Finlay

THE WORLD BANK
Washington, D.C.

Cover paintings courtesy of Rebecca Hind.
Photos in chapter 5: CIRCA Photo Library/John Smith.

Library of Congress Cataloging-in-Publication Data
Palmer, Martin.
    Faith in conservation : new approaches to religions and the environment / Martin Palmer with Victoria Finlay.
        p. cm. — (Directions in development)
    Includes bibliographical references and index.
    ISBN 0-8213-5559-7
    1. Human ecology—Religious aspects. 2. Nature conservation—Religious aspects.
I. Finlay, Victoria 1964–. II. Title. III. Series.

BL65.E36P35 2003
201'.77—dc22

2003057568

For Derek, Cecilie, Jeannie and Patrick,
who in their different ways helped us realize
that the world is an extraordinary place.

Contents

Part 2   The Faith Statements on Ecology

Foreword

The World Bank is committed to the struggle to overcome poverty. At the same time we must protect the biodiversity of the planet. This is an enormous task and one for which the Bank needs as many allies as possible. In the quest for partners who share such goals and who can also bring their own experiences to bear, we need to look beyond the groups with whom the World Bank has traditionally worked.

This is why the World Bank cooperates with the major faiths as partners. In doing so, we follow the example set by the World Wide Fund for Nature (WWF) International. In 1986 the then international president of WWF, HRH The Prince Philip, invited leaders of five of the major faiths to a meeting with leading environmentalists. From this arose a network of faith groups working on ecological and development issues. By 1995, nine religions and thousands of practical projects were involved. In that year, Prince Philip launched a new nongovernmental organization, the Alliance of Religions and Conservation (ARC), dedicated to assisting and enlarging this work. The World Bank was represented at that launch and has been engaged with ARC ever since.

The reason is simple. The 11 faiths that now make up ARC represent two-thirds of the world's population. They own around 7 percent of the habitable surface of the planet, they have a role in 54 percent of all schools, and their institutional share of the investment market is in the range of 6–8 percent. These are serious stakeholders in development. They are also the oldest institutions in the world and possess wisdom about how to live and how to keep hope alive, which we need to hear and respect. So it is very natural for us to work with religious institutions and leaders. The engagement from all sides is one charged with potential and also energized by differences.

In such a fascinating and varied world, full of possibilities but also pitfalls, it is important to have guides who can help chart the adventure. In this book, Martin Palmer guides us, opening up ideas and possibilities that may well be new to many in the world of development and economics, but which, as I know from personal experience, do work.

James D. Wolfensohn
President
The World Bank

Preface

Imagine you are busy planting a tree, and someone rushes up to say that the Messiah has come and the end of the world is nigh. What do you do? The advice given by the rabbis in a traditional Jewish story is that you first finish planting the tree, and only then do you go and see whether the news is true. The Islamic tradition has a similar story, which reminds followers that if they happen to be carrying a palm cutting in their hand when the Day of Judgment takes place, they should not forget to plant the cutting.[1]

There is a tension in the environmental world between those who wish to tell us that the end is nigh and those who want to encourage us to plant trees for the future. In 1992, for example, we were all told, in any number of press statements before the event, that the Earth Summit held in Rio de Janeiro was "the world's last chance to save itself."[2] And indeed many major reports emerging from environmental bodies paint a picture of terrifying, impending destruction—in a sincere desire to shock people into action.[3]

Year after year, these groups have been gathering information that shows beyond reasonable doubt that parts of our living planet are slowly but surely being diminished, polluted, fished out, hunted to the edge, built over, cut down, erased, or—as it is most chillingly expressed—simply "lost." It is increasingly clear, and still shocking, that human activity has assisted (if not created) the increase in global warming; the

---

1. The story is from the *Al-Musnad* of Ahmad ibn Muhammad Ibn Hanbal, written in 1313 and reprinted in 1895 in Cairo. Quoted in M. Izzi Dien, *The Environmental Dimensions of Islam* (Cambridge, U.K.: Lutterworth Press, 2000), 104.

2. The statement was made on a number of occasions by Maurice Strong, secretary general of the United Nations Conference on Environment and Development (the Earth Summit) held in Rio de Janeiro, Brazil, in June 1992.

3. Organizations that have produced such reports include the Club of Rome and Worldwatch Institute, among others.

destruction of many core species of the seas (cod are almost extinct through careless overfishing); the destruction of entire forests within a single generation; and the accelerating spread of deserts. Around the world, hundreds of organizations chart, report, and analyze the declining health of our world and urge urgent action on anyone who will listen. Such groups often fall back on the vivid language of biblical or Vedic (Hindu) accounts of the end of the world—apocalyptic imagery that encapsulates our deepest terrors more graphically than any chart or statistical breakdown can ever do.

Powerfully emotive language is used to make us feel that we are sitting on the edge—that in the words of the Jewish story above, the end of the world is nigh. For example, Maurice Strong, secretary general of the United Nations Conference on Environment and Development, declared in 2000:

> I am deeply convinced that the new millennium we have just entered will decide the fate of the human species. . . . The first three decades of this century are likely to be decisive. Not that we face the prospect of extinction as a species during this period but we will set, irrevocably, the direction that will determine the survival or the demise of human life as we know it. Surely the divine source of all life, which most call God, could not have presented us with a more paradoxical challenge.[4]

If the environmental crises facing the world today were simply a matter of information, knowledge, and skills, then we would be heading out of these dangers. For more than 30 years the world's major institutions, scientists, and governments, and some of the largest nongovernmental organizations (NGOs), have compiled and analyzed details of how we are abusing the planet. Since 1972, huge conventions have brought these people together to discuss the state of the world. Each year the World Conservation Union publishes its Red Data Books, chronicling the loss of species and habitats in great detail. Today we can discuss the issues of global warming in very specific terms. Charts show the destruction of tropical forests, and the loss of crucial habitats around the world is described in books and papers and films.

Yet the crises are still with us. The simple fact is that knowledge on its own is not enough. As the two stories at the beginning of this preface show, all this information has to be set within a wider framework to make much sense. Take, for example, the famous case of the destruction of tropical rain forests. At the first major United Nations meeting on the environment, held in Stockholm in 1972, scientists and environmentalists made powerful presentations on the fact that many countries were

---

4. Quoted in *Survey of the Environment 2000* (Chennai, India: The Hindu, 2000), 15.

selling their rain forests for cash (for reasons of poverty as well as opportunism), only to find themselves left with eroded and impoverished soils. The experts presenting the case assumed that their audience would share their concern at this loss, and stop the deforestation. But that was not the framework within which everyone was listening. A number of politicians and business people went home to their developing countries and informed their superiors that apparently there were groups who would pay good money for all that rain forest—and the rate of destruction of the rain forests rose perceptibly after Stockholm. This was partly because the meeting had opened some people's eyes to the commercial potential of their forests. Both politicians and environmentalists had the same data. But they had different assumptions, different values, and different frameworks.

Ultimately, the environmental crisis is a crisis of the mind. And likewise, appropriate development is ultimately an appropriate development of the mind. We see, do, and are what we think, and what we think is shaped by our cultures, faiths, and beliefs. This is why one of the more extraordinary movements of the past few decades began to take shape. For if the information of the environmentalists needed a framework of values and beliefs to make it useful, then where better to turn for allies than to the original multinationals, the largest international groupings and networks of people? Why not turn to the major religions of the world?

In 1986 this is exactly what the World Wide Fund for Nature (WWF) International did when it invited five major faiths—Buddhism, Christianity, Hinduism, Islam, and Judaism—to Assisi in Italy to explore how they could work on environmental issues. The encounter was so successful that in 1995 His Royal Highness Prince Philip, the Duke of Edinburgh, who was then president of WWF International, launched a new international nonprofit organization, the Alliance of Religions and Conservation (ARC). By 2000 six more faiths had joined the Alliance—Baha'ism, Daoism, Jainism, Shintoism, Sikhism, and Zoroastrianism—bringing the total to 11, with ARC working in just under 60 countries. Its role is to help major faith bodies develop environmental programs and projects, in association with secular bodies as diverse as WWF, the British Broadcasting Corporation, and the World Bank. As part of the Alliance, each of the faiths has compiled its own statement summarizing its relationship with and beliefs about the environment. These statements are presented in part 2 of this volume.

Prepared with the help of the World Bank, this book shows how religions need to be, and increasingly are, in partnership with the environmental and development movements in order to make this world a better place for all life—or, as the faiths more poetically and perhaps more tellingly call it, all creation.

Acknowledgments

None of the work, ideas, projects, or events described in this book would have been possible without the team at the International Consultancy on Religion, Education and Culture (ICOREC) and the Alliance of Religions and Conservation (ARC), and it is a delight to be able to honor the work they each have done. In particular, Joanne Robinson, who ever since Assisi in 1986 has been my key colleague in developing the ideas; Jeannie Dunn, my assistant, without whom nothing worthwhile could happen; John Smith, whose pioneering work on Sacred Land runs through this book; Paola Triolo, whose excellent attention to detail has ensured the success of so many projects; Richard Prime, with whom I have discussed so much over the years; Tjalling Halbertsma, whose astonishing work in China and Mongolia has led the way in helping us see the potential of religious involvement there.

We also owe a great debt to those who help ARC to carry on its work. To Brian Pilkington, Chairman of ARC, whose commitment to the work has been greater than any of us have a right to expect; to Ivan Hattingh and Peter Martin, who first saw the possibilities and gave us such freedom to develop the potential; Rob Soutter, whose inspired idea it was to launch Sacred Gifts; our friends in MOA Japan, whose stalwart support for ARC from day one has been a bedrock on which we have built; Tony Whitten at the World Bank, who has been one of our strongest supporters; and of course, James Wolfensohn, President of the World Bank, whose excitement at the possibilities has been infectious.

Nicki Marrian, Mark Ingebretsen, and their colleagues in the World Bank's Office of the Publisher who worked on the idea of the book and then the editing have been heroic in their willingness to discuss, debate, and revise.

Part 1
Worlds of Difference

1
Changing Worlds

O children of Adam! . . . eat and drink: but waste not by excess for Allah loveth not the wasters. —Holy Qur'an, Surah 7:31

In 1989, when communism fell in Mongolia, there were three registered Buddhist monks. Today, along with the government and the World Bank, Buddhism and the many revived monasteries are a fundamental part of the development and environmental program for the country.

The sounds of the explosions could be heard for miles. Even at night it was possible to spot the giant plume of water shooting up into the air, casting up its bounty into the night sky. Then, like sharks, the little boats would swoop in and trawl up the dead and dying fish—and not just fish. For anything that was swimming in the waters off the coast of Tanzania on those evenings when the dynamite fishermen went fishing, died in the blast.

For centuries, the Muslim fishermen of the Tanzanian coast had fished these waters. Based on islands such as Zanzibar or Masali, they depended on the sea and their harvests for their livelihoods and for the survival of their communities. Deeply religious, these poor communities eked out a living generation after generation. Then someone introduced dynamite. The results were dramatic. For centuries the fishermen had had to hope that they were casting their nets in the right places, deep enough and wide enough to make a decent night's catch. Now, by throwing sticks of dynamite into the sea, they could haul in almost guaranteed catches and it took so little time.

What they did not know (and did not think was their business) was the terrible destruction they were doing, not just to the fragile ecosystem of coral and reefs but also to their own long-term survival. Dynamite wreaks havoc on the delicate balance of nature—of which fishermen are part. It indiscriminately takes out the young fish along with the mature ones, whereas traditional fishing leaves the young to slip through the nets and breed later. The explosion also destroys the very environment within which the fish live. It kills plankton, breaks up reefs and corals, and wipes out the vast array of plant life and other species upon which the shoals of fish depend for their survival. Ultimately, the fish shoals die away and the fishermen and their communities are left with decreasing catches or have to travel much farther out to sea in order to find any fish at all. No one benefits in the long run.

But it was dramatic and fun and for a while yielded high returns. The question therefore became how to help the fishermen understand the long-term problems they were causing, and then stop them. It was the kind of environmental issue that many governments around the world were, and are, trying to address. At first, the Tanzanian government and associated environmental agencies went the usual route: they launched an education program. But like the majority of people in marginalized communities (or indeed perhaps any communities), few fishermen either read or pay much attention to government leaflets, and even fewer looked at those produced by NGO groups, no matter how worthy. Then came legislation: dynamite fishing was officially banned. But again, such communities take quite a pride in ignoring or outwitting such laws. Then a group of scientists, sent by an international body concerned with species loss, arrived on one of the main islands. They brought all their own food and tents and camped out in the wild rather than living with any of the fishing communities. After three weeks spent studying the issue they came to an extraordinary conclusion. The only solution was for the government to have armed patrols capable of hunting down, or at the very least deterring, the dynamite fishermen.

These scientists ostensibly focused on the survival of species, but they made only passing reference to one of the most important species of all: human beings. In part this was because in choosing where they stayed and what they ate they had not made any effort to know the fishermen and their families. But partly it sprang from a strange problem that bedevils certain approaches to ecology and environment: that of ignoring human communities, which are of course as much part of the environment as plants and animals. To its credit, the government only half-heartedly applied the draconian measures—not particularly wanting to shoot its own citizens, even if they were acting illegally. So the problem dragged on. Then a solution of startling simplicity was developed.

The fishing villages of the East African coast are almost all Muslim, and as such they are organized under a religious leadership of sheiks who have enormous authority in the communities. And unlike government officials in far-off capital cities (and particularly unlike well-meaning foreigners from European and American NGOs), the sheiks are very much part of those communities. The basis of the lives of these fishing families is Islam, with its Qur'an, its Shariah laws, and the traditions and customs of the faith. This is what holds the lives of the people together, and this is what provides the worldview that they consider to be paramount.

In 1998, in a joint venture with several NGOs (CARE International, WWF International, ARC, and the Islamic Foundation for Ecology and Environmental Science), the sheiks on Masali island came together to explore Islamic teachings about the appropriate use of God's creation. From these studies the sheiks drew the conclusion that dynamite fishing was illegal according to Islam. They used Qur'anic texts such as "O children of Adam! . . . eat and drink: but waste not by excess for Allah loveth not the wasters" (Surah 7:31). Stories about the Prophet Muhammad's own actions denouncing waste (see chapter 5) were told to convince the fishermen and their communities that what they were doing was against the express wishes of God.

In 2000, the Muslim leadership of Misali and surrounding smaller islands banned dynamite fishing and taught that anyone who ignored this ban risked incurring the wrath of God and endangering their immortal soul. Dynamite fishing was dramatically curtailed. Three years later, in collaboration with scientists and ecologists but guided by the profound insights of their own faith, the communities are developing sustainable fishing. What government laws and the threat of violence failed to do, Islam in partnership with the environmental insights of conservation bodies managed to achieve. And it did so for the simple reason that it made sense within the people's culture and worldview, and it drew not just upon ecological information but on a profound understanding of human nature in the sacred texts.

Whose world?

We all want to change the world for the better. The question is, whose world is it and how can it be changed? We live in many worlds. I am sure you will have had the experience of the differing worlds of the pessimist and the optimist: two people see the same drinking glass, but one sees it as half empty, the other as half full. But it goes much deeper than that. For example, let us take the example of a fox. What do you think a fox is?

To some people, it is simply a reddish-colored mammal; to others it is a classic example of urban adaptation by wild animals; to yet others it is something to chase on horseback. To some animal lovers, the fox is a symbol of the survival of nature against urbanization and the cruelty of hunters; to others, who have fed foxes in their gardens with bread and scraps, it is a beautiful creature appearing almost by magic with its cubs. To cartoon makers and storytellers in many lands, the fox is a wily, cunning creature; to the chicken farmer, the fox is a danger, a predator who can wipe out a livelihood. To Hindus and Buddhists, the fox is a soul just as they are, and may even be someone they knew in a former life. To many Japanese, the fox is a fearful sight, because they believe that evil spirits intent on taking over human beings inhabit the body of this animal.

So let's ask the question again. What is a fox? Our answer has to be: "It depends on what you believe." This is true of everything around us. We understand things because of what we believe. If you believe that hunting is wrong, you will see animals such as the fox, bison, or tiger in one way. If you are a hunter, then you will see them in a different way. If you like sausages, then you will see the pig in one way. If you are a vegetarian, you will see the pig somewhat differently. If you believe the world is there to be used as you want and when you want, then you are not likely to treat it the same way as someone who believes it is the loving manifestation of a Divine Being or that all life is itself part of the Divine.

What you believe gives meaning to what you see. It determines how you use, treat, and respect the rest of the world. The challenge to those seeking to make the world a better place is how to help different visions and different experiences of the world to work together. If you do not realize there are different worlds, but insist everyone should see the world as you do, you can lose key potential allies who feel their world has been ignored. Seeing and respecting other worlds opens up vast possibilities.

Two versions of a forest

The coastline of Lebanon has been massively developed in the past 20 years. Towns have spread north and south, creating an almost unbroken line of urbanization along the seashore and covering the hills behind with vast stretches of concrete homes and roads. At times, driving along the coast can seem like driving on a long highway cutting through suburbia. As a result, the natural environment of the Lebanese coast is under unprecedented pressure. It is one of the most dramatic examples of something that is happening all around the Mediterranean: the coastlines are being built upon, destroying rare ecological systems and running the risk that the Mediterranean will soon be a sea ringed by concrete.

In response to this rapid development, the United Nations Environmental Program and other environmental agencies identified the Mediterranean coast as a priority for preservation and set up a task force to help it. WWF International counts the survival of Mediterranean shrublands and woodlands on its list of the 200 most important world ecosystems to be protected. Aerial photos taken in the late 1990s highlighted the degree to which development had already reduced shrublands and woodlands in countries such as France, Greece, Turkey, and, perhaps most dramatically, Lebanon. The one bright green spot of hope was discovered to be a sizable ancient forest north of Beirut covering three hills. The researchers from the task force were surprised and delighted to discover this remaining block of forest, the forest of Harissa, and immediately took steps to ensure its protection.

They contacted the landowners of this rare and crucial forest, and sent them a 48-page scientific, economic, and legal document demanding a promise to abide by national and international laws to ensure the protection of the forest. In the worldview of the people in the task force, these laws and the weight of the scientific evidence were paramount. They wanted to do good and were anxious to help the landowning organization fall into line with the good that they wanted done. They got no reply. It took the wisdom of a local environmental group led by a Druze and a Maronite Christian to work out why.

The forest of Harissa belongs to the Maronite Church of Lebanon. The church has owned this forest for centuries, perhaps as long as 1,500 years. Its priests and decision makers were not ignorant of the forest's beauty and environmental importance, but it had a deeper significance for them. It is known as the Holy Forest of Our Lady of Lebanon, and at its heart is the Cathedral of Our Lady, with a giant outdoor statue of the Virgin Mary, whom many see as the Protector of Lebanon. Yet in the document from the task force—written in that strangely unappealing language that so dominates the utterances of the environmental movement and scientists—no mention of the forest's spiritual, cultural, historic, and emotional significance was made. Its authors simply did not see that world of the Harissa forest, and as a result they were unable to communicate with the Church and its followers.

A new approach was needed. ARC and WWF already had a program called Sacred Gifts for a Living Planet, designed to recognize commitments to the environment made by communities based on people's religious traditions and their beliefs about the natural world.[1] Protecting the sacred Harissa forest seemed to be an ideal example of a Sacred Gift. With this in mind, representatives of ARC and the local Association for Forest Development and Conservation (AFDC) went to meet the head of the Maronite Church. The palace of His Beatitude the Maronite Patriarch lies within the sacred forest of Harissa itself. Within half an hour the

---

1. WWF and ARC summarized the notion of a Sacred Gift as "a practical, concrete and active expression of a religious tradition and its belief about the natural world. This initiative will honour what is already happening and through specific Gifts will indicate significant new commitments." From the Sacred GTTE Checklist pertaining to voluntary forest protection, WWF/ARC, November 12, 1999.

Patriarch had committed the Church to protect the forest in perpetuity. By drawing upon the Church's sacred understanding of the forest and experiencing the world through the insights of Maronite theology, culture, and tradition, the decision—and pledge—made sense locally as well as internationally.

It is worth comparing the first document sent to the Church, which they ignored, with the document the Church later drew up with the help of AFDC and ARC. The differences between the documents reflect the huge differences between the two worlds, even though both share a common concern and now a common commitment to protect this rare forest. The following dictatorial definition of why the task force thought the Church would want to work with it is a classic example of a view of human nature, commitment, and intentions that sees the glass as half empty:

> Dedication to biodiversity protection—i.e. is the area especially dedicated to the protection and maintenance of biodiversity and associated natural and cultural resources?
>
> To satisfy this test, the area's custodians must have protection of biodiversity as a first order management objective. If other objectives take precedence over biodiversity protection, then the area as a whole, or those parts of the area where other objectives take precedence, should not be classified as a protected area. Forests managed for other environmental functions, such as soil or watershed protection, will not qualify as protected areas where these other functions are higher order objectives than maintenance of biodiversity. Forest areas dedicated to environmental protection functions other than biodiversity should be distinguished from protected areas and labelled differently (e.g. as protected forests).[2]

In contrast, this is how the Maronite Church expressed its commitment to protect the forest and its "biodiversity," and perhaps more important, why:

> For centuries the Church has defended the natural beauty and Godliness of the forests and hills of Harissa, as well as so many other holy places in Lebanon. . . . In so doing, we observe that the land and the flora and fauna on it, do not ultimately belong to us. We are simply the guardians of what belongs to God. It is in this spirit that the Church has for centuries protected such sites as Harissa. But today, new threats endanger this holy site and so many others. Harissa is now surrounded by the growth of buildings and just as the Basilica [cathedral] is a boat floating on the mountain

---

2. From the document endorsed by the WWF Core Forest Advisory Group, October 1999.

so Harissa floats like a ship of nature above the tide of modern development. Therefore the Church must speak boldly and make clear to all that the Holy forests of Harissa will remain, protected, managed and owned for God by the Church. . . . It is this conviction which leads us to consider the forests of Harissa registered under the name of the Maronite Patriarchate as a Maronite Protected Environment of Harissa.

In protecting this area, the Church will continue to ensure that the diversity of plants, trees, animals and birds given by God, nurtured by the Church will be maintained. . . . We are aware that not only does the world need to know why we are making this clear statement, but our own faithful need to understand that this action springs from our faith. St. Maron [the fifth-sixth century hermit saint after whom the Church is named] sought God in the wilderness of creation, amidst nature itself. Today, in the spirit of St. Maron we need to rediscover why God wishes His Church to care for nature, through education, through teaching and preaching. Through looking again at the life of St. Maron and the thousands of hermits who sought Christ in the forests and valleys, we can become true believers, caring for all aspects of God's creation.

That is why the forest is now protected formally as well as spiritually. That is also why, since the declaration of the protection of the forest in 1999, the Church has created an ecology center for young people and parishes in a monastery, protected two other major woodland sites, and developed a program of environmental education and action in 77 villages and towns, becoming one of the key advocates of environmental protection in Lebanon. Because they believe in it. How sad it would have been if these two worlds—that of the evangelizing environmentalists with their awareness of the importance of this forest in the wider picture, and of the Church with its tradition of protection which needed reawakening—had not been able to meet. By insisting that people adopt their view of the world, many campaigning groups cut themselves off from natural allies, who may see things differently but no less compassionately.

Seeing many truths

Many people are actually rather scared of being told that their worldview is just one among many. We like to think that unlike so many others, we see "the real world." Yet the world we see is a construct of our minds, our backgrounds, our training, and our assumptions. The world is, thank goodness, bigger, more exciting, and more diverse than that which we alone see.

A British friend of mine tells a story about how her worldview was turned upside down. She was 19 and spending a university summer teaching math and English in a Tibetan refugee camp in India. She was living in one of the children's homes, with about 20 children and a young housemother. One evening she was sitting with some of the children, telling them stories and singing songs before they went to bed. A bedbug crawled up her bare ankle and she casually squashed it against her skin. And then she looked around and saw the unmistakable expressions of horror on the children's faces. "It was as if they had seen me pick up a kitten and strangle it while in the middle of a song: it was a horror of casual violence that was beyond their comprehension." At that point my friend realized that the way she had seen the world was not the only way. After that summer she switched her university course from economics—"which was just one way of seeing human behavior, a way that I wasn't sure I believed"—to social anthropology, so she could understand the concept of pluralism that she had seen so vividly.

Most people in the West grow up with the notion that truth is monolithic: that there is only one true way to explain how the world evolved—evolution—and only one true faith, whether that is Christianity, Islam, atheism, or something else. In the West we tend to want there to be one pathway and one right answer, whether this is "one true way of democracy" or "one true model of economics" or "one true way of bringing up your children" or "one true way of dealing with terrorism." But the rest of the world sees this as rather childish and not very helpful. I found this out on my first visit to India, when I was in my early twenties.

I was working with people of different faiths—Hindus and Jains and Muslims—helping them develop educational resources so that European schoolchildren could learn how their religions worked and what they meant. At a personal level this caused me some confusion. If Christianity were true—as I had been culturally taught—then the others de facto could not be. Yet I was moved by much of what I was seeing. I raised this problem at a meeting with Indian Christians. They gently pointed out that perhaps it was not "the other religions" that were the problem, but me! It was my assumption that my tradition was ultimately the best and therefore only serious model that was the problem. It had nothing to do with other people's different beliefs and ways of seeing. "Relax," they said. "God is bigger than your thoughts, greater than your models and wiser than your philosophies. Relax and listen."

It broke apart my inherited worldview—thank goodness. It forced me to see that maybe I was the problem. It is like this for all of us. We have to have a worldview, otherwise we cannot function. As Carl Jung wrote, we have to inhabit a worldview that explains most things for us because if we didn't "we would be crushed by the sheer awe-ful-ness of the universe." The problem comes when we think that this is actually the only reality, or that it is any more than a helpful way of looking at something that is actually rather complex. The world is so much more exciting than that, and in order to make it a better world we need to realize this and then create structures that enable diverse and even conflicting worldviews to work side by side.

Constructing a future

An illustration of how worldviews can differ is provided by the extraordinary story of the rebuilding of the statue of Avalokitesvara in Mongolia. From 1924 to 1989, Mongolia was a communist country. Indeed, after Russia, it was the second country to go communist. The government committed all the terrible actions of Soviet communism, including the suppression of religion: in the purges of the 1930s and again in the 1950s tens of thousands of Buddhist monks were murdered and virtually all monasteries destroyed. A few were kept as museums, and in 1989 just one monastery in the capital city Ulaanbaator was kept open as a "functioning" monastery to show visitors from abroad that religion was not oppressed. It is said that by 1989 there were just three monks allowed to work openly.

Mongolian people have traditionally believed that their country is under the protection of a deity called Avalokitesvara, who is the Bodhisattva of Compassion. In Buddhism, Bodhisattvas are beings who— through countless lives of exemplary goodness—have reached a point where they can slip the physical ties of rebirth and escape to Nirvana, never again having to suffer the troubles of existence. Yet these enlightened beings decide instead to help other souls escape the cycle of rebirth. Of these compassionate beings, Avalokitesvara is the most loved.

In 1911 Mongolia gained its freedom from the Chinese, and one of the first things its people did was to cast a 26-meter-high statue of Avalokitesvara in bronze. In the 1930s Stalin ordered that the statue be destroyed, and legend says it was shipped in pieces to Russia where it was later melted down to make bullets for the war against the Nazis. In 1989 there was another huge shift in Mongolia's history. Communism collapsed and out of the mess arose a democratic movement. In this first noncommunist government was a young politician named Enkhbayar, who headed the Ministry of Education—or as it was called in those heady days of freedom, the Ministry of Enlightenment.

The country was in disarray. Poverty, poor housing, the aftermath of forced collectivization, and settlement of the nomads meant the country was convulsed with problems. The euphoria of the fall of communism was soon replaced by the grind of making a new society. Aid agencies and intergovernmental bodies poured in with advice, plans, schemes, projects, and programs—as well as funding. They all knew what needed to be done: new educational priorities, development models, criteria for funding and sustainable growth and so forth. Yet what happened took them all by surprise, and—for those who were able to understand—it revolutionized their understanding both of Mongolia and of how to rebuild a country.

Enkhbayar and other key ministers decided what they needed to rebuild first, and made a public announcement to that effect. No outside agency would touch this project, considering it a waste of time and money. Yet ordinary Mongolians poured money in, giving what they could, even if it was only a few coins. Relying upon Mongolians themselves, rather than on international help, the project became the focus of social, political, and spiritual life in Mongolia and gave thousands pride and hope.

And what were they building, when they needed schools and housing so badly? They were remaking the 26-meter-high statue of the Protector of Mongolia, Avalokitesvara. From the worldview of the aid agencies it had at first seemed a colossal waste of money, yet from the worldview of so many Mongolians it was a massive success and the beginning of a new era. As Enkhbayar (now prime minister of Mongolia) explained, without pride in themselves or the sense that they were once again protected, how could the Mongolians move on? What had he to offer his people if they did not value themselves? With foreign aid he could provide more schools, projects, and funds, but what would they be worth if people did not have a sense of who they were?

The statue changed everything. It also changed the worldview of not a few aid agencies with respect to what it is that helps people make sense of the world and thus change it. The world has so many more dimensions than many of us think, and the engines of change and of making the world better are so fascinatingly diverse as soon as you start including different worldviews. In this book we will celebrate this diversity, as well as offering models that show how—far from needing to be resolved by one grand plan—this diversity can work.

The World Bank and other faiths

This book is the product of a most unusual informal working relationship between ARC and the World Bank, which began in 1995 when ARC was launched. Each of the participating faiths was asked which contemporary secular phenomena they felt could be most important in helping, or hindering, the work of the faiths on the environment. Two came out clearly: the mass media, especially satellite television, and modern economic thinking, embodied for many of the faiths in the modus operandi of the World Bank. This is why at the launch of ARC the World Bank was present in the person of Andrew Steer, then the head of the Bank's environmental department. The debates, discussions, and even disagreements that arose from that initial encounter were enough to encourage the faiths to accept an invitation from the World Bank to take the contacts further. The fledgling ARC was asked to coordinate this from the faiths' side, and this led to a series of meetings in London and Washington over the next two years between ARC staff, religious leaders, and the World Bank.

In February 1998 the first full formal meeting was held between religious leaders and the leadership of the World Bank.[3] Since then ARC and the Bank have developed closer links through, for example, the involvement of World Bank staff such as Kristalina Georgieva, Andrew Steer's successor, at the ARC/WWF International Celebration of Sacred Gifts for a Living Planet held in Nepal in November 2000.[4] Here, World Bank, ARC, and religious representatives met to discuss practical projects to be undertaken together in countries such as Mongolia, Cambodia, and Indonesia. More recently, an initiative between the World Bank and ARC has begun to develop management plans for forests in Romania that have been handed back to the Orthodox Church. World Bank staff and leaders have attended a variety of ARC events, such as the meetings to create the International Interfaith Investment Group, or 3iG (see chapter 4) in New York in June 2002 and London in November 2002, and the Royal Celebration of ARC's work in November of that year. Likewise, ARC staff have spoken at World Bank conferences and have joined various meetings at the Bank to present the religious perspective. Together ARC and the World Bank have also assisted events such as the interfaith meeting in Bogor, Indonesia, in December 2002 and the launch of ARC/World Bank/WWF projects in Mongolia in May 2002.

Work with ARC represents one of the ways in which the World Bank relates more and more to the worlds of the religions as it seeks to broaden the network of groups with which it works. The focus of the ARC/World

---

3. This conference, which was organized by ARC and co-chaired by the Archbishop of Canterbury and President James Wolfensohn of the World Bank, led to the formation of the World Faiths Development Dialogue. This research body met again in Washington in November 1999 and Canterbury in October 2002. Its mandate is working on development priorities such as education, health programs, post-conflict resolution, and gender issues. Environment and natural resource management are explicitly not included—ARC is the body working on environment and natural resource management from the faiths' perspective with the World Bank.

4. The involvement was made possible through a grant from the World Bank–Netherlands Partnership Program, Biodiversity/Forest Window, to the World Bank East Asia and Pacific Environment and Social Development Unit. This grant led to the creation of the Forest and Faiths Initiative.

Bank involvement is naturally on the environment, though through initiatives such as 3iG (see page 41) this expands to embrace general issues of ethical investing, land management, and poverty reduction.

There are still many people within the religions who are suspicious of the World Bank, and many within the World Bank who have no idea what the Bank is doing dealing with such obscurantist bodies as religions. Yet despite this, and perhaps because of the types of stories told in this chapter, this partnership is working.

In 1998 ARC held a meeting with a major international financial body set up to assist development and sustainable growth. But for some people in the financial organization, this meant that the work should be done on their terms only. This was vividly brought home by one man who spoke to the team at the reception afterwards. He was delighted, he said, that the world religions were being brought together. He looked forward to them agreeing to the same thing and behaving in the same way because he was a statistician and the anomalies that different faiths created really messed up his statistics. He will be disappointed by this book.

Diversity is the building block of change. From the language of evolutionary science, we know that diversity is crucial to the development of life on earth. Only through diversity can you have the variety that ensures that when one dominant species collapses or when one kind of environment gives way to another, new species and ecosystems can emerge to continue the journey of life on earth. If this is so for creation, then I would argue it is true for humanity as well. We need diversity because all models, all beliefs, and all systems fail. Without diversity we would not have the intellectual and practical wherewithal to tackle problems that we cause through our own beliefs and systems. Without diversity we could not evolve.

I go back to the gentle lesson I received from the Indian Christians. Both my world and my God were too small. My problem was not out there: it was inside me. And what is true for an individual is equally true for institutions and communities—including of course the great religions. So why and how did we end up with such small worlds to inhabit, and what, if anything, can we learn from the experience of the world's oldest institutions about the nature of permanence and change? This is the subject of the next chapter.

2

How Did We Get Here?

Ahimsa—this is a fundamental vow and runs through the Jain tradition like a golden thread. It involves avoidance of violence in any form, through word or deed, not only to human beings but to all nature. It means reverence for life in every form including plants and animals. Jains practice the principle of compassion for all living beings at every step in daily life. Jains are vegetarians. —The Jain Statement on Ecology

In the last 150 years the major religions of the world have suffered more persecution, more deaths and destruction of their sacred places by ideologies opposed to religion, than throughout the whole of the rest of recorded history. Yet the faiths are still here . . .

So how did we get to think so small?

The West has a particular genius for creating (and then seeking to spread) systems of belief that cannot stand other systems of belief. Where this was once thought only to be true of missionary Christianity, we can now see it at work in just about every other form of ideology that has originated in the West. Take Marxism. Marxism is a Western creation: it was built on a Judeo-Christian worldview, but its Truths, by which everything is to be seen and judged, are not based on spiritual values but on economic laws and the inevitable march of history. The worldwide spread of Marxism involved a deliberate attempt to destroy existing beliefs and value systems—whether religion, feudalism, or even basic capitalism. Its intolerance of competitors is one of its most disturbing characteristics.

Capitalism likewise finds little space for competing value systems. And in order to destroy them it invokes not revolution but quasi-divine powers called "market forces," which are allowed the sovereign right to remove, ignore, or override other value systems. Even the many people who wish to change the world for "humanitarian" or environmental reasons sometimes suffer from a blinkered vision of the rightfulness of their values and beliefs and the need to impose these upon others in order to do them good.

I was recently shown a copy of a proposal drawn up by a very respectable international environmental group. It was a plan based on the knowledge that the gases emitted by cattle can contribute quite considerably to global warming. The proposal was to persuade nomadic people in the Central Asian steppes to agree to have their herds of cattle killed. And in return for having their traditional way of life trashed in the name of preventing global warming, the nomads were to be offered solar-powered TV sets by the environmental group.

Somewhere along the line someone had lost sight of the plot. Or, more disturbingly, they actually did believe that in order to make the world a better place a traditional way of life had to be broken and replaced by a consumerist, television-based worldview. And they believed that it was fine to start with targeting poor, vulnerable communities that could be bribed, rather than the huge multinationals—automobile manufacturers creating car exhaust, for example, or the dairies and burger chains with their vast cattle production—that contribute so massively to global warming, but have stronger lobby groups than the nomads. The proposal, incidentally, did not receive funding.

The common trait of all these movements—whether Marxism, capitalism, or environmentalism—is their desire to make a different world, a world that they would all claim to be better, but that involves everyone else becoming and thinking "like us." Yet most people in the world have lived with pluralism and diversity for millennia and they see no such need for one absolute world vision. The roots of this primarily Western desire to make everyone think and behave in the same way lie deep in history, and they have shaped not just how the West reacts, but increasingly how all the world reacts.

On one level, it all started on a dark night in Athens in the late fifth century B.C. On that evening the young philosopher Plato and his friends went on a rampage. Through the night they tore up and down the streets of the city attacking the statues of the gods that lined the roads, placed outside people's homes to protect the families. The reason for their hooliganism was that their teacher Socrates had taught that the profusion of "gods" and "goddesses" was a smoke screen hiding the reality that all Truth and all Divinity is One. Socrates taught that there were no gods or goddesses and ultimately there was only one Mind, one Divine Force, behind the whole of existence. This belief in the monad—the absolute and unemotional Oneness behind all existence—has been the core model in the West ever since, and in the spirit of Plato and his friends, those seeking to convince others that there is only One Reality have been breaking other people's statues ever since.

In the West we have great difficulty accepting that diversity has any real role in the world. Remembering Socrates, there is a feeling that either there is only One or there are the Many—there cannot be both. As a result, both religious and secular missionary movements arising from this monad model have over the centuries sought to convince the world that there is only one way forward, one truth, and one reality. Theirs.

It found its early manifestation in the Pax Romano—the political policy of the Roman Empire—and then found another vehicle in Christianity, with its claims of absoluteness and its rejection of other faiths as false. This model held sway until it was challenged in the eighteenth century by the rise of the new absolutes of nationalism and revolution, followed by yet more absolutes: socialism, Marxism, capitalism, industrialization, science, economics, fascism, and so forth. All of these purport to be concerned with making a better world, but all seem to carry with them an intolerance of any values other than their own.

One world, many worlds

Not long ago, a group of very eminent environmentalists, economists, and other people concerned with the future of the world held a meeting to discuss what they called a "new ethic." Talk of this new ethic had been popular for some time, and arose from a sincere desire to try to make the world a better place by creating an ethical code—a code that could be seen as binding upon everyone, whatever their religious background. It is a fine ideal, and also potentially a highly divisive one.

At the meeting sat a lone Hindu representative, a scientist. When it came to dinner on the first night, after a day of exhaustive and exhausting discussion about common codes of morality and ethical structures for enforcing ethical behavior, the Hindu raised a little question. Why, he asked, was meat being served for dinner? The others reacted badly and asked in return why he was raising such a question. "Because," he said, "in my tradition, ethics means not eating a living creature."

Many people who want to make the world better, such as the earnest new ethics group above, act like latter-day evangelists. They know what is good for the world, and they are intent upon helping us to do what they know is best whether we like it or not. En route, views, beliefs, values, and even ways of life that don't fit get at best ignored. At worst, the new missionaries actually try to destroy such beliefs and ways of life, as in the story of the Central Asian nomads, where the plan was not only to break the herding life but to replace it with the banality of TV.

In the struggle to persuade the world to accept a model of absolute truth a great deal else has been crushed. And ever since the age of ideology began with the French Revolution of 1789, one of the main targets has been religion. This was for good reasons as well as bad. Absolute power corrupts absolutely, and any system that has almost total control will go bad. Medieval Christianity in Europe, eighteenth-century Islam in India, Tibetan Buddhism in the late nineteenth century, or militant Sikhism in the twentieth century are all examples of what happens when religion has the power to exercise almost full control. No religion has escaped debasement by human greed, stupidity, or ambition, and by the time of the eighteenth century in Europe much of religious life was a sham. It needed to be broken in order to reform.

But as so often happens, the baby was thrown out with the font water. All aspects of religion were soon either condemned by revolutionary movements or consigned to irrelevance, often by relegating them to the realm of "private choice" or "individual conscience." Furthermore, what began as a sincere desire to break the stifling hold of corrupt religion—as in eighteenth-century France—soon became a desire to break religion altogether because the new ideology wanted to take its place, power, authority, and wealth.

By the mid-twentieth century religion was being physically persecuted in nearly one-third of the world, from the Soviet Union through China and Mongolia to Mexico. Elsewhere (including in the major countries of Europe) it was increasingly sidelined, with its ancient networks of schools and welfare institutions and its role as pastoral caregiver increasingly being taken over by the state. Religion had also been relegated to the sphere of the mind. Science and in particular psychology had largely displaced religion in the intellectual firmament. Up until the eighteenth century, religion provided the dominant model of reality through which people saw, understood, and related to the world. Even at the beginning of the scientific revolution (often linked to figures such as Isaac Newton) religion still provided the framework within which the new scientific discoveries made sense. This is rather nicely borne out by the mock epitaph for Isaac Newton, written by the English poet Alexander Pope around 1718:

Nature and Nature's laws lay hid in night:
God said "Let Newton be!" and all was light.

By the mid-twentieth century, such a cohabiting of God and science was largely unimaginable. Religion was seen as the enemy of science, or at least as having once been relevant but now displaced by the discoveries of science. Many people forecast that religion would soon be extinct, except in those areas of "backwardness" where modern economics, science, thought, philosophy, politics, and society had yet to make any significant impact.

At the heart of all these changes lies the same attitude that led Plato and his mates to go on a destructive rampage: intolerance and fear of diversity. What has made this intolerance even more dangerous than the youthful Plato is that so many of the new ideologies have contended that their model was the only one that could make the world happy and thus legitimated the destruction of those who stood in their way. Yet despite predictions to the contrary, religion is not dying out. In some places—including Britain—it is struggling, but in other places it is burgeoning. For example, the first book published by the World Bank on faith and development was focused on the Church in Africa, where, it pointed out, most of the poor are deeply religious. Indeed, the Christian Church has grown fivefold in Africa over the last 40 years.[1]

Today, this simplistic but destructive way of thinking is changing. The work of the World Bank in partnership with religions is a classic example of this. Until recently the World Bank has not been known for its tolerance of diverse social and economic models. Indeed it has tended to operate with a single model of economic truth that it maintains would ensure the good life for all—if only followed properly. One book even described it as a "faith."[2] But today some senior decision makers in the World Bank are actively seeking diverse models and no longer feel that there is a Truth that has to be applied come what may. This nascent change in thinking is also evident in increasing numbers of people in the environmental movement.

The World Bank and other development organizations have been greatly affected by the increasing discussions (both internally and externally) of a broad agenda around ethics and development. Some of these themes were exemplified in an exhibition on cultures, religion, and ethics at the International Monetary Fund headquarters in Washington, D.C. The exhibition opened in September 2002 and was organized and inspired by the work of Hans Küng.[3] Partly as a result of the tragic events of September 11, 2001, and in an effort to reach out to a wider audience of social actors and civil society organizations, the World Bank and many other institutions are attempting to delve deeper into issues

---

1. The book, *Faith in Development*, was based on a meeting sponsored in 2000 by the World Bank and the Council of Anglican Provinces of Africa on alleviating poverty in Africa. It was attended by senior Bank staff who spoke not just on the economic and social aspects of development, but also on the spiritual aspects. The focus of the meeting was poverty, but the communiqué included the statement that "[w]e are committed to protecting the natural environment." See D. Belshaw, R. Calderesi, and C. Sugden, eds., *Faith in Development: Partnership between the World Bank and the Churches of Africa* (Oxford: Regnum; Washington, D.C.: World Bank, 2002).

2. Susan George and Fabrizio Sabelli, *Faith and Credit: The World Bank's Secular Empire* (London: Penguin, 1994).

3. See Hans Küng, *Tracing the Way: Spiritual Dimensions of the World Religions* (New York: Continuum, 2001) and *World Religions: Universal Peace, Global Ethic* (Tübingen, Germany: Global Ethic Foundation, 2002).

that are deeply embedded in the central mission, culture, and values of development.

The fear of diversity is beginning to give way to the recognition that no single model can ever do justice to the breadth and depth of human experience or possibility. This breakdown of reliance on "the One" is what is now making it possible for some of the various worldviews that have survived for centuries to begin to find a way of contributing together for a more pluralist future. Christianity, for example, is a classically monolithic model—but much of contemporary Christianity has begun to develop a theology of pluralism. "Ecumenical" is a key word, and Christianity is now one of the most active faith groups in the interfaith world. Moral certainty can be a very dangerous thing and can blind its followers to the true nature of their role. A fascinating example of this comes from the Jains.

Looking anew at old beliefs

Jainism arose in India at the same time as Buddhism, around the sixth century B.C. Its fundamental teaching is ahimsa—nonviolence—and it is taken so seriously that even today Jain monks and nuns will gently sweep the floors in front of them to ensure that they do not harm even an ant. The strict teaching of ahimsa led the Jains to forswear any trade that involved taking any form of life. So they moved out of agriculture, leatherwork, meat production, and so forth and instead looked for trades that involved inanimate objects. Even today Jains dominate in the fields of mining, gem dealing, and petrochemicals.

In 1991 the Jains applied to join the original WWF International network on conservation and religion. But they got a shock. Proud of their ancient tradition of ahimsa, they were confident that their impact on the natural world was gentle and positive. But when they actually checked, they found they were mistaken. In terms of environmental protection, mining, the exploitation of gems, and the development of petrochemicals are among the most damaging activities. By concentrating on what they did not do—hunting, meat production, and agriculture—the Jains had not really looked at the impact of what they did do. Their ahimsa principles, which led them into mining and petrochemicals in the first place, were actually being undermined by the contemporary practices of these industries, now increasingly destructive to the environment.

In response to these insights, the Jains set about tackling this issue with their customary aplomb. They created an annual award for the Jain-run industry that had done most to mitigate its harmful impact upon the natural environment, and they began to look at ways in which their involvement in such industries could be pro- rather than anti-environmental. It will take time and it will not be easy, but guided by their worldview the Jains will change and will make a significant difference to the future of the world.

This is only possible because, once again, an ancient religion is challenged and allowed to return to its roots in order to find a way forward. As the next chapter will begin to show, it is exactly this pluralism that is the way forward for a world in which monolithic worldviews have had their day. We have thought small for a long time. Now it is time to think big, and think more widely and wisely.

3

Changing Minds

*Daoism has a unique sense of value in that it judges affluence by the number
of different species. If all things in the universe grow well, then a society
is a community of affluence. If not, this kingdom is on the decline.*
—The Daoist statement on ecology (chapter 10)

According to the World Bank study Voices of the Poor, *the poor trust their
religious organizations more than any other institution with the exception of
their own social institutions.*

The crisis was a severe one and the invasion seemed unstoppable.
They flew in by the millions and brought almost total devastation in
their wake.

It was the early 1970s and the brown plant hopper had arrived in
Indonesia. This small insect was sucking the rice crops dry. In previous years the crops had increased dramatically as a result of massive
use of pesticides and the introduction of irradiated rice. For the rice
plant–sucking hopper this was a paradise, and hoppers were now at
plague levels of infestation: previously each insect would lay three
eggs a day, now they were laying 10, and Indonesia was facing a possible famine. It was at this point that Professor Ida Nyoman Oka, then
a professor in the agriculture faculty at the Gajah Mada University in
Jogjakarta, became involved.

The Ministry of Agriculture needed professional advice. By this they
meant scientific advice. However, after a great deal of thought, Professor Oka—who also happened to be a Hindu priest—and his Hindu colleagues called on their knowledge of religious lore as much as of
agriculture. They recalled the story in which a good king tries to kill a
wicked demon king, but whenever he cuts off a head, two spring up in
their place. In Hindu lore, the good king wins by remembering the moral
principle of not killing.

23

And so did Professor Oka. He persuaded the desperate government to try a new approach, one that did not rely on chemical warfare. And in the end the brown plant hoppers were defeated not by using new weapons but simply by stopping the use of pesticides at all. This "passive resistance" allowed many other species to recover. Once the insect's natural predators—other insects and spiders—had returned to normal levels, they took care of the brown plant hopper and the balance was restored.

The lesson from this experience was that the great religions have learned more about how to really work with the problems of the world than some of the "missionary" environmental groups who often have solutions but perhaps not always wisdom. Sometimes it is only by remembering what we really believe in that we can change our underlying behavior in relation to the natural world. This approach is reflected in the projects that the World Bank and ARC are supporting.

In this chapter we will look at how the religions help to change minds, and we will also see what we—as people who care about the earth, whatever our spiritual beliefs may be—can learn from them.

First of all, the role of religion in helping people change how they think and therefore behave is something that many would see as a contradiction in terms. The popular perception of religions in the secular world is that they are unchanging and unyielding. Yet the extraordinary fact is that religions survive *only* when they adapt to new circumstances, and this is what the successful world religions have been doing for more than 2,500 years. The unsuccessful ones, for example, the Stonehenge culture of Bronze Age Britain, were the ones that were unable to adapt—and they are either extinct or at least on the endangered list. Only faiths that could be flexible have remained.

To cite another important example: In the Middle Ages, European Christianity had become deeply corrupt. Then the trauma of the Black Death in the mid-fourteenth century shattered the notion of the Church having "negotiated a deal with God." The old sense of security that people had in their faith was in tatters. But Christianity survived. The Reformation and the Catholic Counter-Reformation response were radical rethinks of the whole of religion in Europe, which meant that by the late sixteenth century two virtually new modern versions of Christianity had emerged, replacing the medieval version. The faith had survived because it had adapted.

And here we have one of the secrets of success of religions: they know how to seem timeless and yet how to shift with the times. This is one of the ways in which they have shaped all the major cultures of the world throughout history: they have stayed relevant. Religions—at their best—manage to combine change with authority, and they define new moods and shifts in perception rather than just jumping on the bandwagon of any passing social trend. After all, according to the World Bank's major study of poverty, *Voices of the Poor*, poor people trust religious organizations more than any other organizations except their own social institutions.[1] As the Indonesian story about the plant hoppers highlights, over the centuries religions have learned a thing or two about nature and our place within it, as well as a thing or two about human behavior.

What we need now are more opportunities for these insights to be heeded and understood. And if they are indeed understood and then acted upon, this will benefit the environment, local communities, and also the religions themselves, some of which are at critical points in their own histories. To show how religions often have something important to contribute to the environmental debate, I will give the example of the Daoists in China, who are helping solve a critical environmental problem—with a solution that almost nobody in the secular world had even imagined.

Saving tigers with philosophy

Traditional medicine has a history in China that stretches back at least 2,000 years. Although rooted in ancient knowledge, it nevertheless has been a key part of Chinese modern medicine since 1949, when Mao Zedong declared that medicine should walk on "two feet"—meaning China should use both traditional and Western scientific ways of healing. The strategy mostly worked and in recent years traditional Chinese medicine has become very popular outside China as well. Today, virtually every major city in Western Europe has its Chinese medicine shops and clinics. The demand for the products, primarily prescriptions, has rocketed. This, combined with the huge increase in spending power of people in China, has created a huge demand for the traditional ingredients.

Mostly this is not a problem; indeed it is probably beneficial. But certain prescriptions have had a devastating effect on wild species. For example, tiger penis and rhino horn are key in a number of popular prescriptions for impotence; tiger bone and bear gall are supposedly linked to strength. The demand for these ingredients has led to illegal hunting and trapping, or cruel "milking" of bears for gall. And it has pushed several species to the very brink of extinction. The Chinese government has made many of these ingredients illegal, but the trade is continuing. The

---

1. D. Narayan, "Voices of the Poor," in Belshaw, Calderisi, and Sugden, *Faith in Development*. Also see D. Narayan, *Voices of the Poor*, 3 vols. (New York: Oxford University Press for the World Bank, 2000–2002).

trouble is that there are many illegal or unofficial practitioners: some are charlatans but many are heirs to ancient lineages of healing practice. It is these people—and their clients—who need to be reached. This was where the Daoists came in.

Chinese medicine is based upon an understanding of reality different from that of Western medicine. Its worldview is based on belief in the Dao—the nature of the universe—which is best described in a famous series of verses in the Dao De Jing, written in the fourth century B.C.:

> *The Dao gives birth to the One:*
> *The One gives birth to the Two:*
> *The Two gives birth to the Three:*
> *The Three gives birth to every living thing.*
> *All things are held in yin and carry yang:*
> *And they are held together in the qi of teeming energy.*[2]

The One is the universe, which gives birth to the two primal forces of yin and yang, which are the natural forces of opposites. Yin, for example, is cold, wet, winter, female, and earth, while yang contrasts to this by being hot, dry, summer, male, and heaven. They are locked in perpetual combat, yet—as their classic symbol shows—each contains the seed of the other. So while autumn and winter are yin, they inexorably give way to the yang spring and summer, which in turn give way to autumn and winter and so on. These Two give birth to Heaven, Earth, and Humanity, which give birth to all living things, but with humanity given the role of balancing everything else. And all life—including human—is said to be motivated by the power of the breath that animates each of us, known as "qi."

Traditional Chinese medicine builds upon these theories by saying that to restore health in a sick person, one needs to reconnect him or her with the natural flow of life. Illness comes from an imbalance of yin or yang and a subsequent crippling of the qi—which is how the ingredients of medicines are decided.

Although Daoism is the philosophical gatekeeper of the traditions underpinning Chinese medicine, curiously no one had thought to approach the Daoists to help deal with the current problems. In part this was because the Chinese government was embarrassed by the religious-philosophical basis of Chinese medicine, and in part it was because the Western scientific bodies tackling the issue saw the problem as one of education and science, and didn't appreciate the spiritual theories that underpinned it. There is also a real problem in that the growth in use of traditional Chinese medicine is now often unconnected to its original

---

2. Chapter 42 of Dao De Jing (Tao Te Ching), adapted from the translation by Man-Ho Kwok, Martin Palmer, and Jay Ramsay (Shaftesbury, U.K.: Element Books, 1997).

roots, for it has become a major industry—and this industry has been the target of most work on making traditional Chinese medicine more environmentally friendly. However, in such a struggle, all potential allies need to be developed and this is what has happened with the Daoists.

Once the Daoists were alerted to the problem, they offered some highly practical and yet also deeply philosophical answers. First they went back to the core of traditional Chinese medicine and concluded that any medicine that either endangered a rare species or caused undue suffering to animals was doomed to be a failure.[3] How could you cure one species by destroying another, or by inflicting terrible pain on another part of the universal Dao?

In 1999 the Daoist Association of China issued an edict excommunicating any traditional medical practitioner who uses prescriptions that contravene the laws of balance. But prohibition was only one part of the solution. Daoist scholars and healers then set about researching, from their vast library of ancient medical texts, alternative prescriptions that did not involve endangered species. It is a strategy that might contribute to solving the enormous problems that the growth and increasing "industrialization" of traditional Chinese medicine have created. Practitioners are likely to pay more attention to a teaching that not only shows them why their medicine won't work but also offers them a traditional alternative, than they would to a government edict. But even more importantly, Daoists are not operating as remote scientists. These scholars already have contact with, and the respect of, unofficial traditional medicine practitioners—many of whom live close to temples or on or near Daoist sacred mountains.

In this example the Daoists were asked only to explore the ancient basis of traditions that were proving to be damaging to the environment. What actually happened was that a new dimension of Daoist teachings emerged, rooted in tradition but addressing a contemporary issue. It is an example of how all religions move forward while maintaining ancient truths. But religions have other strengths as well that we can learn from. Because alongside the ability of faiths to reinvent or reinterpret themselves lies an extraordinary ability to convey complex social ideas through simple stories—stories that people remember.

Telling wonder-ful stories

For example, consider the all-important notion of compassion. Many parents, teachers, governments, and activists want to encourage the people around them to be kinder, gentler, and more thoughtful to others. In many countries, children are now taught a class called "citizenship"

---

3. *China Daoism*, November 1999 (in Chinese).

which is supposed to inculcate good behavior. Meanwhile—with a strange echo of nineteenth-century missionary activities—some of the more earnest environmental groups have tried over the last 15 years or so to develop a notion of a new world ethics: a code of good behavior which they say everyone ought to follow.

But few of these secular approaches recognize a basic tenet of human behavior: telling people what is good often leads them to do exactly the opposite. For example, in the United Kingdom, it was found that programs designed to stop children smoking or being racist often actually encouraged them toward this behavior. For the young people it suddenly offered them a way to thumb their noses at Authority. So, then, how can anyone effectively share the vision of a more compassionate world, in order to encourage other people to want to be part of it? There are ways of doing it without moralizing.

Religions, of course, have been as guilty of moralizing as anyone else, but they have also learned that the best, perhaps the only, way to pass on a truth or insight is through humor, storytelling, mystery, and awe. Take, for example, the Islamic teachings of caring for people less fortunate than yourself. The following story is one of the most beloved of stories, one that takes the listener into a wonderful world of compassion—not by exhortation, but through a sense of mystery.

Once upon a time, the story goes, there lived in a great Muslim city a man called Ahmed. All his life he had been saving up for his once-in-a-lifetime trip to Makkah for the pilgrimage of Hajj. Every Muslim who can is supposed to make the long, arduous pilgrimage to Makkah in fulfillment of one of the main teachings of Islam. He was not a wealthy man and Makkah was a long way away, but over the years he had managed to save enough money and now the time was coming for his departure. A group of his friends were also going and the night before they were due to leave they gathered at his house to celebrate the beginning of their adventure.

After they had all left, Ahmed and his family went to bed. But sleep was not to last long. Early in the morning a fire broke out four doors away and Ahmed and his family rushed to help their friends.

They found a terrible scene of destruction and distress. The family had lost almost all their belongings, and their house was nothing more than a pile of smoldering wood and stone. So Ahmed offered his house and set about helping rescue what could be retrieved from the fire. As a result, when his friends came at midday to collect him he told them to go ahead and he would catch up with them within a day or so. So they went off, urging him not to take too long.

But it took nearly a week before the neighbors' situation was under control and Ahmed had to spend some of his savings. Just as he was ready to go, a young mother of three children, whose husband had died a year before, also died. Ahmed realized that someone had to help the children find a loving home. He spent three days sorting this out and once again found he needed to use some of his saved money to solve the children's problems.

By now, it was getting almost too late for him to catch up with his friends and his money was stretched to the limit. Still, he packed his bags and prepared to leave. This time he got half a day from the city when he found a man who had been robbed, lying by the roadside. Bringing him back to the city, he paid for him to be treated by a good doctor and offered him hospitality in his own house.

It was with a sad heart that Ahmed realized it was too late to go to Makkah. Furthermore, he had only very little of his hard-earned cash left. He felt a failure, as if he had somehow let God down. But there was nothing to be done about it.

Two months later his friends returned with great rejoicing and came straight to Ahmed's house. When he opened the door he immediately apologized for not having come to Makkah and having let them down. They stared at him wide-eyed. "What do you mean?" they asked. "We saw you there." They saw his astonishment and continued, "Yes, you had the place of greatest honor and we wondered why."

The power of such a story is that it draws you into the narrative (and leaves you to draw the conclusions) while imparting core beliefs and values of Islamic life and teaching. It is a way of involving people that businesses, for example, have tried to make use of in commercials, and that secular environmentalists would do well to pay attention to.

Long-distance thinking

The symbolic nature of religious actions offers a powerful model for changing the world—in manageable steps but, importantly, *with a long-term view*. Quite often in ARC we are asked to join a "crucial" or "vital" campaign on some vast issue such as management of forests or protection of the seas. We are invited to throw all our weight and connections into a campaign only to discover—just as we have got the impetus going—that another "priority" comes along and the former "vital" campaign is over.

Religions take time to move but when they do, they make commitments for a very long time. For example, in many cities and towns the only surviving green patches are those surrounding old places of worship. If you visit Tokyo, for example, and look down from the train as it sails over the city en route from the airport, you will see that it is only around the old Buddhist or Shinto temples that any greenery survives: often ancient trees or small ponds struggling on in the midst of the concrete. In Istanbul, it is the old churches and mosques that provide the green lungs: around the famous mosque of Eyup, the ancient trees that have been preserved because it is a sacred cemetery are the last breeding place of storks on the Golden Horn. In Bangkok, a similar story is to be told: the wats, or Buddhist temples, provide vital green spaces not just for smog-weary citizens but also for many species whose habitats have otherwise been destroyed.

In the United Kingdom, a scheme to exploit this phenomenon of urban survival was launched in the late 1980s. The project was called "the Living Churchyard," although it was not so much a vision of the dead rising up as of the dead providing sanctuary for species whose living space had been so cut back. Now more than 6,500 British churches run their little plots of land as "sacred ecosystems"—without pesticides, and mowing the grass only once a year—ensuring that a number of species of birds, reptiles, insects, and bats can thrive.

This is an example of turning something that has always existed—the local churchyard—into something that embodies the Church's core teachings about respecting nature. The scheme has been outstandingly successful for several reasons. First, because it immediately makes sense; second, because it is simple to execute; third, because it is theologically sound; and fourth, because it enables millions of local people, through their churches, schools, and community groups, to become involved in a manageable environmental project.

From this one program there has now sprung a whole code of conduct—built upon protecting the ecology of what is often called "God's acre"—not only for graveyards but for the management of church lands in general. It has taken nearly 15 years for all this to begin to develop its potential, but once a pattern of land management is established, it will remain part of "how we do things in the Church" for many years to come. Until, indeed, it is time to adapt again.

The second example of long-term thinking offers an even greater time scale. In Sikhism, time is measured in 300-year cycles. In 1999 Sikhs moved into their third such cycle. The first two cycles had been named as they began, and although the names were inspired by events just before each new cycle, they also shaped the spirit of that cycle. For example, the years between 1699 and 1999 were called the "Cycle of the Sword," because in the late seventeenth century the Sikhs were fighting for their lives against the Mughal Emperors who had invaded India; the Sikhs decided to fight back not just for themselves, but to protect all the weak and vulnerable. The Cycle of the Sword ended with a terrible civil war in the Punjab, when Sikh militants sought to create a separate state and the Indian government crushed them.

As they approached 1999, the Sikh leaders wanted a very different theme for the next 300 years. At the time ARC was working very closely with the Sikhs on developing land management and alternative energy schemes. Through our discussions, the idea arose of naming the new cycle the "Cycle of the Environment" or the "Cycle of Creation." This was agreed by the whole community and now the Sikhs have made a 300-year commitment to focus on the environment. What does this really mean? Well, one early benefit is that many Sikh temples now hand out tree saplings as a sign of blessing to worshippers instead of a sticky sweet. It is estimated that 10 million saplings are being distributed every year, making up the woodlands and gardens of the future. Religions can make commitments like this because they think in the long, long term and have the experience of having done so for a long, long time.

Having seen how religions work over extended periods, communicate through stories, and change minds by reminding people what is most vitally important to them, I want to show how environmentalists (both faith-based and secular) can put this learning into practice in order to care for nature.

Work with what you have; perhaps it is enough

Often all that is needed is to shine a new light onto a traditional practice for its significance to become relevant once again. Take, for example, Islam's recovery of its ancient codes for ecological management.

So many trees have been destroyed in Indonesia that Java has now lost all of its lowland forest, and statisticians tell us that unless there is a massive effort to stop the logging, Sumatra will be in the same position by 2005. In response to this crisis, and urged on by a joint ARC/World Bank program, some Javanese Muslims are recovering ancient traditions of protection of trees—traditions that have lain dormant and almost unnoticed within Islam for centuries. Building upon this, Islamic leaders, working in collaboration with conservationists from the Botanical Garden of Indonesia, have started to develop a "new tradition" among rural Islamic communities in upland areas to appoint a "guardian" of each hill or mountain.

This is no fanciful spiritual position: these village-appointed sheriffs are responsible for monitoring their local area for logging and other damaging behavior. "It appears already that state forestry companies and police are heavily involved in illegal logging," said Kyai Thontowi Musadda, the cleric who started the scheme. Once the local communities realized that protecting the environment was part of Shariah, or Muslim law, they not only began to demand the resignation of the corrupt officials but also slowly became active protectors of the mountains themselves, giving new life to an Islamic tradition that is more needed today than it was when first promulgated.

Likewise, in Thailand, environmentalists involved with the Buddhist Protection of Nature project have helped Thai Forest monks identify a tradition of protecting the forests. The fact is that where there is a monastery or even just a simple monk's dwelling, the forest surrounding it—for 5 or even 10 miles—becomes sacred. It cannot be logged for fear of upsetting the monks and the Buddha or the many forest deities associated with rural Buddhism. By making a decision to choose to live in endangered forests, the Forest monks can be active environmentalists even as they meditate.

In both the Indonesian Muslim case and the Thai Buddhist example, nothing new has been created, but old traditions have been given a new role and meaning. This has happened because the religions have opened themselves up to meet the environmental, scientific, and political groups struggling to make a better world. Without the challenge that comes from these largely secular forces, it is doubtful that the faiths would have undertaken these activities. Yet without the faiths, the chances of the secular forces ever actually effecting serious changes in human behavior are slim.

Finding allies

In 1986 His Royal Highness Prince Philip, then president of WWF International, suggested that for the conservation movement to have any real chance of success, it needed to find allies who could help spread the message and engage people in the struggle to save the earth. And so he took the unprecedented step of inviting representatives of five religions—Buddhism, Christianity, Hinduism, Islam, and Judaism—to join with the key environmental movements in exploring what the various teachings had to say about caring for creation. The meeting was held at Assisi in Italy, the birthplace of St. Francis, the Catholic saint of ecology. And the reasons for its importance were spelled out by Prince Philip in his opening speech:

> We came to Assisi to find vision and hope: vision to discover a new and caring relationship with the rest of the living world, and hope that the destruction of nature can be stopped before all is wasted and gone. I believe that today, in this famous shrine of the saint of ecology, a new and powerful alliance has been forged between the forces of religion and the forces of conservation. I am convinced that secular conservation has learned to see the problems of the natural world from a different perspective, and I hope and believe that the spiritual leaders have learned that the natural world of creation cannot be saved without their active involvement. Neither can ever be the same again.[4]

---

4. *Religion and Nature Interfaith Ceremony* (Gland, Switzerland: WWF International, 1986), 42.

It is this changed vision, this wider worldview, that lies at the heart of serious change, and for this to happen all of us—religious and secular—have to encounter some worlds that make us uncomfortable, as well as others that excite us with new ideas, models, and visions.

Prince Philip was not preaching entirely to the converted. To most people, even those who were present at Assisi, this idea of the forces of religion and conservation coming together sounded very odd indeed. To many of them, religion was either something they thought was no longer particularly relevant to the modern world, or something they thought was a private matter. Yet as we have shown, whatever our own spiritual beliefs, religions do have lessons that make a lot of sense, and that we could all benefit from hearing. Some of them are predictably about how to be good, some of them are about how to be effective, but one of the most important lessons is—perhaps surprisingly—about how not to be too pious. Indeed it is about how to party.

Protect the earth—and ourselves

One of the saddest features of the activist world—be that environmental work, peace work, or whatever—is the phenomenon known as "burnout." So many activists throw themselves so deeply into their activities to create a better world for others that they end up exhausted. Here again, religions have been there before them—and might be able to offer some advice.

There is a moving story of St. Francis that sheds some light on this. Francis was a visionary, totally committed to the service of all creation in the name of God. He allowed no possessions, either for himself or for his other brothers in the early Franciscan movement. They were not even allowed their own prayer books. In 1210, Francis traveled to Rome to present the Pope with the Rule for his new religious movement. But to his astonishment the Pope refused to authorize the Rule. In great distress, Francis begged him to explain. The Pope said that while he had no doubt that someone as driven as Francis could live by the extreme laws he had drawn up, as Pope he had to consider those who would not be able to give everything every day with no thought of themselves. He asked Francis, in compassion, to draw up new rules that could be honestly lived by ordinary mortals—that would not, in modern English, lead to burnout. Francis did so and the vision of the Franciscan Order, which has inspired so many millions, was created. It was created out of compassion as well as out of passion.

Religions know that you cannot just make demands on people: you have to give as well, allowing people to celebrate as well as repent. The great faiths embody this in the cycle of each year, and there are many lessons to be learned by looking at how religious calendars are broken up into manageable portions, offering a variety of times, spaces, and thoughts for the year. In Christianity, for example, the high points of the year are marked by both fasting and feasting. Fasting is important because it reminds people of the need for self-restraint, for times of thoughtfulness and reflection which are aided by having an outward sign—fasting—of an inward spiritual journey. But the fasts, Lent and Advent, for example, are immediately followed by feasts—Easter and Christmas. These times of feasting are times to celebrate life and its abundance, its wealth and its joys.

Islam has a similar pattern with the fasting month of Ramadan followed by the fun of Eid-Ul Fitz, and in Indonesia this has been linked to ecology in a program being developed by the World Bank to produce a series of daily reflections on the environment for Muslims. These will be distributed to radio stations and newspapers around the country during the Ramadan fast, with a suitably exciting environmental celebration scheduled for Eid.

The need to acknowledge the limits to what any one individual can do, and the need to have fun and relax, are vitally important truths for any group or movement seeking to change the world for the better. There are two Jewish sayings that highlight this. The first is that on the Day of Judgment, you will be judged and condemned for all the legitimate pleasures you could have enjoyed but did not. The second saying is that on a death bed, no one has ever said, "You know, I wish I had spent more time at the office."

Understanding the importance of balancing the need for repentance with the need to party is a central insight into human psychology that the faiths can bring to the environmental and developmental movement. And similarly, the very human art of setting goals while recognizing that sometimes those goals are only to be striven for in order to discover a deeper truth is also central to all the faiths.

Let me give a personal example. For a long time I have had a special interest in the divine feminine element both in Christianity and in Chinese religion. In Chinese religion she is manifest in the stories, statues, and person of the popular goddess Guanyin. She is the female form of the Bodhisattva of Compassion, Avalokitesvara, whom we met in Mongolia in chapter 1. The focus of her tradition is her sacred island and mountain of Putuo Shan, which lies some 30 miles off the eastern coast of China near Shanghai. I have wanted to visit this place for a long time. But I have never made it. Each time I have tried, the trip has been cancelled. For a while I was getting a bit desperate and feeling as if I was fundamentally failing to achieve. Then I came across a phrase by a sixteenth-century Buddhist master. He put everything into perspective for me by writing that "You don't have to go to the East Sea to meet Guanyin.

Putuo is in your mind."[5] The faiths would argue—and their way of living usually bears witness to this—that to change the world you need to change yourself and that only from this will flow that ability to see the world differently which is the very heart of change.

The stories above are all about taking what is best within a tradition and giving it a new meaning in a different context. They are also about having a sense of the wonder of life that is often, sadly, missing. Groups seeking to improve the world too often come across as worthy, dull party-poopers. This is as true for the secular world as it is for the more puritanical elements of the religious world. Part of the challenge the mainstream elements of the faiths bring to the environmental and development movement is the worldview that this is a wonderful creation, loved by God and held in compassion by the divine. That alone is worth celebrating, as it is every morning in, for example, the morning prayers of the Catholic Church or the pujas of Hindu devotees.

A worldview that sees only the worst and most depressing traits of human society doesn't inspire or excite anyone else. It might frighten them, but terror is not a good basis for a worldview. Religions have been as guilty as any group of using scare tactics to try to get commitment. Visit any Buddhist temple in, say, Sri Lanka or China and you will find the 18 hells of Buddhism graphically depicted on the walls, intended to scare people into good behavior. Or listen to a fiery Christian or Hindu speaker talking about the torments awaiting the soul. But these approaches are more fringe than many outsiders appreciate. Much more fundamental is the fact that through religions, people down the ages have celebrated births, marriages, birthdays, special events, beloved saints and gurus and have dealt with death, sorrow, pain, and betrayal. Religions honor the mundane sacredness of everyday life.

In November 2002, at the request of Prince Philip and as a gift to Queen Elizabeth II for her Jubilee Year, ARC hosted a "Celebration of Creation" at the Banqueting Hall in London. Representatives of each of 11 major religions participated with prayers and music, dance, and even a tranquil garden created for the day.[6] The event was called a celebration because there was so much for which to give thanks: that the environmental movement has begun to resist the destruction of our planet, and that side by side with them, all the major faiths are taking up the challenge of protecting creation as well.

---

5. Quoted in Martin Palmer and Jay Ramsay with Man-ho Kwok, *Kuan Yin: Myths and Revelations of the Chinese Goddess of Compassion* (London: Thorsons, 1995).

6. The 11 faiths that are members of ARC are Baha'ism, Buddhism, Christianity, Daoism, Hinduism, Islam, Jainism, Judaism, Shintoism, Sikhism, and Zoroastrianism.

The religions celebrated that day because for all faiths, creation is wonderful, mysterious, profound, and hopeful. One of the greatest sacred gifts the faiths can offer is hope: hope that through the insights of the environmental movement and the faith of people worldwide, we can begin to reverse our destructive role and create something beautiful with nature.

And as I have shown in this chapter, one of the first steps in that reversal is to apply some of the ways that religions can teach us how to change destructive mindsets. These are:

- Telling wonderful stories—a subject I will return to in chapter 5
- Thinking and acting in the long term, rather than considering only the next election or funding cycle
- Looking at what we have already in terms of wisdom, and applying it to new problems
- Working hard, but not too hard
- Celebrating what we have, rather than just crying over what we have lost.

The transformation of individuals has to go hand in hand with the transformation of institutions. In the next chapter we explore one of the most ambitious (yet also achievable) examples of how institutions can also change individuals.

4
Investing in the Future

No one lighting a lamp puts it under a basket, but on a lampstand and it gives light to all in the house. In the same way, let your light shine before others, so that they may see your good works and give glory to your Father in heaven. —The Bible (Matthew 5: 15–16)

More than one in six of the world's population are Catholics.

A t the height of the Great Terror in 1935, the French foreign minister suggested that Josef Stalin should take Catholicism seriously. The Soviet leader derisively replied: "The pope? How many divisions has he got?"[1] The answer, of course, was none—popes no longer have armies. Yet ironically a few decades later it would be a pope—John Paul II—who helped bring down the empire that Stalin built so ferociously. Furthermore, while the pope may not have an army in the conventional way he is head of the largest single voluntary organization in the world: the Catholic Church, with more than 1 billion followers worldwide and an influence to match.

This chapter shows how, in the struggles to create a better world, the potential "divisions" or "battalions" of the faiths have been largely ignored—or perhaps they have been invisible, even sometimes to themselves. It also argues that one religion or NGO or even the biggest bank in the world can have only a limited impact on its own—and that if we are really going to help support biodiversity, humans need to recognize, live with, and ultimately make use of our diversity in beliefs, experiences, and resources. This is acknowledged in the Millennium

---

1. Quoted in Winston Churchill, *The Gathering Storm,* vol. 1 of *The Second World War* (Boston: Houghton Mifflin, 1948), chap. 8.

Development Goals adopted at a United Nations summit in September 2000 and promoted by the World Bank.

Katherine Marshall, director of the World Bank Development Dialogue on Values and Ethics, puts the first point very well:

> The world of religion has been an unacknowledged and often unseen force for many development practitioners in the past. Many reasons, both good and bad, explain this divorce; hard-won traditions of separation of state and religion are deeply ingrained and deliberately place a remove between development and faith issues. . . .
>
> The suggestion that religion is important for development and the converse, that development is important for religion, and hence that dialogue between religious institutions and leaders and their counterparts in development institutions should be enhanced, has jarred a goodly range of people. The two worlds are often seen as far apart; religion deals with spiritual matters, whereas development is very much in the material world. It takes little reflection to advance past this first reaction, but the initial take has significance; it highlights the vast differences in the perceived worlds and also the emotional reaction that bringing them together can stir.[2]

However, there are encouraging signs that the secular world is waking up to the significance of the religious. For example, in a speech to the World Bank in March 2003, the Taoiseach (prime minister) of Ireland, Bertie Ahern, said he offered

> particular praise for faith-based, or missionary, orders who for decades have provided education and health for countless thousands of poor, including many of today's African leaders. Ireland's missionaries have played a crucial role in the development of many African states. Their work has provided the foundation for our close bonds with many of our African partners. As our overseas aid budget increases, we are ensuring that our support for missionary orders also increases. I agree with [World Bank President] Jim Wolfensohn that in addition to their development work, the churches have brought an ethical and spiritual dimension to development cooperation based on their moral authority which makes them crucial partners in development.[3]

It is a welcome statement for many faith-based environmentalists— but it is still unusual enough to attract attention. And the problem is not just with the secular bodies. Religious communities have not really taken stock of their true influence either.

---

2. Katherine Marshall, "Development and Religion: A Different Lens on Development Debates," *Peabody Journal of Education* 76, no. 3/4 (2001): 339-75.

3. Bertie Ahern, "Globalization, Partnership and Investment in People: Ireland's Experience" (speech to the World Bank, Washington, D.C., March 13, 2003).

Discovering spiritual currency

In 1999 ARC started to develop an asset audit of the major faiths: we wanted to see how much they were worth financially. We thought some of the bigger faith bodies at least would know the assets they had. But most of them did not. Perhaps the most interesting example of this happened in Nashville, Tennessee, at the initial meeting with the United Methodist Church. This Church is the fourth largest in the United States, and has some 11 million members. It is organized into 66 "conferences" across the country and has well-developed boards dealing with ministry, education, women, social affairs, mission, publications, pensions, and so forth.

At this first meeting we met heads of the key boards who told us one by one what they were doing on environmental issues. Eventually we came to the Pensions Board representative, Laurie Mickalowski. She informed us that her board had a socially responsible investment program, which meant that virtually all the pension funds were ethically monitored, and the board sought to move funds into socially responsible areas and companies. Impressed, we asked how much the Pensions Board handled in terms of its investment portfolio. And when we learned that it was around $12 billion we were even more impressed. We then asked what the total stocks and shares portfolios of the entire Church were worth. No one knew. But we were invited to go away for a few months while they worked it out. A few months later the answer arrived.

The United Methodist Church in the United States had holdings of around $70 billion. (By comparison, the Church of England holds nearly one hundred times this amount.) We found similar stories among other groups: massive funds, some socially responsible investment, and great potential for doing more. What we had discovered, almost by accident, was the immense financial clout of the major faiths. It is a power that has not been used in a concerted way, and indeed it is a power that to a very great extent the faiths are almost shy about.

There is a traditional embarrassment about the relationship between (to use Christian language) God and Mammon—which has meant that the faiths have been somewhat reticent in exploring their actual stakes in the physical, economic, and social life of the world. The faiths have not really sought to flex their financial muscle, yet many of them have assets far greater than many banks or multinationals.

In understanding the role of the major faiths, we need to think in terms of major businesses and not see that phrase as in any sense derogatory. And we need to look at some very big numbers. The Catholic Church, for example, claims over 1 billion members—one-sixth of the world's population. It has a full-time staff of 1.5 million priests, monks, and nuns. That figure can be increased to over 20 million if the teachers who work in Catholic schools (including partly state-funded schools as in the United Kingdom, schools that are part of a denominational state system as in Germany, and schools that are private as in the United States) are added to the list. There are also 500,000 or so lay people working as social workers or youth workers or administrators in Catholic-related roles worldwide.

In terms of buildings—including churches, monasteries, retreat centers, schools, parish halls, sports facilities, publishing companies, media centers, research centers, and universities—the Church owns something in the region of 1 million structures. In many countries the Catholic Church provides the welfare net to catch the most impoverished and the most needy. And in countries such as Italy, Brazil, Germany, and Spain, it also runs the majority of the historic buildings—the churches and cathedrals that are the very heart of the national tourism trade.

How does it pay the wages of all those people? It cannot rely on the dollars, euros, and pounds that go into the collection plates on Sundays, although they help. The answer is that the Catholic Church supports such a vast empire of staff, services, and facilities through its shares, stocks, and other assets. It is in effect a business, or more accurately a series of businesses, with a huge portfolio of investments held locally, nationally, and internationally.

By looking at the Church in this way we can begin to understand this faith group's potential for serious action on environmental and developmental issues. Many NGOs and international bodies are desperately trying to build themselves constituencies, capacity, and networks, but the Catholic Church already has all of that in place. It is present in virtually every country, and in almost every town and village in many countries. It has 141 ambassadors accredited to its headquarters in the Vatican—an indication of the seriousness that many countries accord to relationships with the Church. It also, as we have seen, has a great deal of money and investment power. In this light, the decision not to take seriously such a vast and proven multinational business does seem rather naïve. Yet the traditional attitude of so many secular groups to the Church is that—in some way they find difficult to articulate—it is "no longer relevant."

Sikhism is another good example. In India, where 82 percent of Sikhs live, the Sikh community of 13 million maintains some 28,000 temples known as gurudwaras. Each gurudwara runs, as an essential part of the temple complex, a "langar" or free kitchen where anyone—regardless of need, creed, or caste—will be fed. Day in and day out the Sikh community, from its own resources, feeds anyone who comes. It is an extraordinary gesture: the community as a whole feeds about 30 million people a day, with the five great gurudwaras of Delhi feeding more than 10,000 people every day. The energy consumption for such an undertaking is vast and the social significance impossible to overstate. Millions of people survive in India because of the Sikh gurudwaras. Add to this the role of schools and other welfare institutions such as clinics and care centers, and we are looking at a major national enterprise without which India would be greatly the poorer.

Again, such a huge undertaking needs careful financial management. The contributions of the faithful are managed as large portfolios and invested in business ventures before they come to be invested in food for hungry people. Without the accountants, the spiritual and welfare work of the Sikhs could not continue for long. Yet, as Katherine Marshall of the World Bank pointed out at the beginning of this chapter, these immense resources have not been taken seriously and—as we found—even the faiths had not really appreciated their potential role for using their financial as well as spiritual clout to make the world a better place.

International interfaith investment

In November 2000 there was a historic meeting in Kathmandu between representatives of major faiths and the environmental and development worlds. They agreed to support the creation of what would be an international interfaith investment group, named "3iG,"and ARC was asked to undertake its organization. It is one of the best examples of what can happen when different worlds meet and agree to find ways of working together that not only respect the differences, but actively build upon them.

Following the debates at Kathmandu, the key mission statement for 3iG was that each faith should assess its portfolios with "due regard to [its] beliefs, values, the environment and human rights so that all life on Earth can benefit." Most of the faiths had already established clear moral policies about what they should *not* invest in: few would buy shares in tobacco companies, distilleries, gambling organizations, arms manufacturers, or companies they perceived to support blatantly unethical governments. But although several had also supported vital incentives such as microlending—giving small loans at tiny interest rates, often to village women—most had not thought about using a large part of their funds to invest in ventures and companies with beneficial social and environmental impact. 3iG is designed to assist the faiths in encouraging and supporting this development and to provide first-class research and information.

How could they afford to do this? The faiths are almost unique in having a long-term perspective on investments, while the general market often has to think shorter term. Even though they have to make good returns on their investments in order to keep on going, they do not have to take all the profits tomorrow. Increasingly, however, the short-term outlook for such investments is also favorable. Ethical investments are being seen by the commercial world as significant because of their sustainability: on a simple level, if a company is efficient enough to conserve energy and take steps to protect the environment, it is probably efficient enough to do its business successfully.

In June 2002, finance officers from different faiths met in New York to begin developing a model to lead to the creation of 3iG as an independent body to which all faith fund managers and financial officers could relate. The new group is being set up to manage religious funds—but as well as its religious advisers it also has a secular advisory group that includes Citigroup, Rabobank, and the World Bank, as well as agencies such as Innovest and WWF International and economic think-tanks such as Medley Global Advisors.

This project is a good model not only of how secular and religious worlds can cooperate, but also of how the differences between and within religions can be developed positively, through what 3iG calls "cluster groups." For example, with advice from WWF and the World Bank as well as their own advisers, the faith groups in 3iG have decided to focus their innovative investment on a few key areas, one of which is alternative energy. At the moment new projects in this area often lack development funding, and so are vulnerable to the efforts of existing energy providers to stop their plans. To break out of this "poverty trap," the alternative energy movement needs an estimated $700 million in research and development. One single faith group, even if it has a portfolio as big as the United Methodist Church's, cannot afford to put this amount of money into research and development. But 3iG is currently working with faith investors to create a cluster group to take up this challenge. This is not out of a sense of charity. As we have seen, the faiths have to make good returns on their money in order to pay their bills, but these returns do not have to be as instant as other investors would require, and the faith groups can afford to look at businesses that give significant returns over the long term *and* might possibly help make the world a better place.

The cluster model, which developed from ARC's own working practice, enables faiths to collaborate when they want to while keeping full autonomy. It allows diversity (rather than unanimity) to be a core value. Groups can identify key issues for themselves and then seek partners to work with them. So, for example, Islamic, Daoist, and some Christian investors might join together to provide microfinance to poor communities developing sustainable products, and they might do so on a non-usury (no-interest) basis as this reflects their specific beliefs and values. Or Hindu, Jain, and Zoroastrian (Parsee) investors might cluster around water investment in India.

This pluralism gives the kind of flexibility that many faiths now see as the best way forward in developing their relationship with the rest of the world. It is a flexibility that is reflected, for example, in the National Religious Partnership for the Environment, a Jewish-Christian alliance based in Amherst, Massachusetts. Embracing the U.S. Catholic Conference, the National Council of Churches of Christ, the Coalition on the Environment and Jewish Life, and the Evangelical Environmental Network, the partnership is an example of many faiths in one country working together on social and environmental issues.[4]

Another important aspect of the interfaith investment model is what has been called the "cascade" effect. Each faith in 3iG has agreed to pass on information about the socially responsible investment policy to its followers. This effectively means that believers will be told about their religion's investment policy—and will be encouraged to invest their own personal funds in socially responsible ways. This cascade effect takes faith-inspired, socially responsible investment to a completely new level. Take the United Methodists again: their own pension fund is $12 billion. But their active congregations include between 5 million and 7 million families. Citigroup estimated that each family probably has investment savings (in the form of pensions, equities, bonds, and so on) of $50,000 to $75,000—which means that the estimated constituent fund of Methodist faith members is between $250 billion and $500 billion.[5] Even in the clipped language of banking investment managers, the potential impact is clear.

The 3iG model is one of the more dramatic examples of the interaction between religious worlds and secular worlds. Let me give some more modest examples to indicate how bringing worlds together can amplify the contribution of each in ways that they could not achieve alone.

Saving the vultures

The first example is the problem of the disappearing vultures of Mumbai in India. For the Zoroastrians (known in India as Parsees because they originally came from Persia), the disposal of the dead is crucial. Central to their teaching is respect for the Seven Bounteous Creations— sky, water, earth, plants, animals, humanity, and fire—and the sense that

4. See appendix 2 for a list of groups working with faith and environment.

5. Michael Even, "The Market Impact of 'Faith-Consistent' Investing" (paper presented at ARC/3iG Conference, New York, N.Y., June 19, 2002).

human beings as the purposeful creations of God, are the natural overseers of these Creations.[6]

But according to Zoroastrian teachings, the dead human body is ritually (and actually) polluting. It cannot be buried for this would dishonor
earth; it cannot be burned because this would dishonor fire; it cannot be
thrown into the river or sea because this would dishonor the waters. So
the Zoroastrians build Towers of Silence. These extraordinary structures
stand in the center of downtown Mumbai and elsewhere in India and
Iran where Zoroastrian communities live. The bodies are laid out on
these towers and left for the vultures to pick clean, after which the bones
can be gathered and disposed of.

The trouble is that there are not enough vultures left in Mumbai to eat
all the dead Zoroastrians. This is due to air pollution, loss of habitat, and
the fact that the city has become cleaner so there is less for the vultures
to scavenge. The loss of vultures is a serious problem and has been
addressed by a unique partnership. The Parsees have linked up with
specialist bodies, such as the natural history section of the Prince of
Wales Museum in Mumbai and various international bodies concerned
with protection of vultures, to develop an intensive raptor-breeding program. So that this is not just a selfish project, they are also assisting vul-
ture-breeding programs around the world to share information and
knowledge so that these extraordinary birds, which have had a bad press
but which are vital for the disposal of carrion, can be preserved.

The lost sutras of Mongolia

Meanwhile, in Mongolia, an unusual project combining both old and
new wisdom has developed in collaboration with the Buddhist communities, the government, WWF, the World Bank, and ARC. Following the
collapse of communism in 1989, Mongolian Buddhism was able to
emerge from underground, where it had been driven by terrible persecution. It has now begun to rebuild its role as one of the foundations of
Mongolian life, culture, and identity. The country is undergoing rapid
development, which is necessary to ensure a decent standard of living
for its citizens. Yet the inappropriate development of so many countries
in the past 50 years has served as a warning, and has caused the government to try to find a new model. Part of this involves looking at the
past and at ancient writings about the sacred nature of Mongolia.

---

6. As the Zoroastrian statement on ecology says: "The great strength of the Zoroastrian
faith is that it enjoins the caring of the physical world not merely to seek spiritual salvation, but because human beings, as the purposeful creation of God, are seen as the natural
motivators or overseers of the Seven Creations." See chapter 17.

Gandan Monastery, supported by several international agencies, commissioned a book entitled *Sacred Sites of Mongolia* which gathers together ancient texts or sutras that mention sacred places. Many of these sutras were thought to have been lost under the communists. They not only list the sacred mountains, rivers, and valleys, but also set out rules for the survival of the delicate ecology. The book's introduction says:

> One of the major reasons for working with the traditional religion of Mongolia is that buried deep within it are legends, stories, even names which tell us a great deal about a proper relationship with nature. . . . For many outside Mongolia it might seem strange to look to the names and legends of the past to build a new future. But Mongolia has a delicate ecology, which has been respected—indeed venerated—throughout history because people instilled in names and legends wisdom concerning the correct and appropriate use of such places. In an era of rapid change such as that which confronts Mongolia at the start of the 21st century, we need to know how to walk gently upon this fragile land and the past tells us how.[7]

Through legends telling of how a mountain goddess will send landslides to those who cut down trees in her sacred forest, or of river deities who will send floods if the area is stripped of vegetation, the Buddhist sutra writers and their shamanic forebears pointed out the adverse effects of deforestation and overgrazing on fragile floodplains in ways that were intelligible to the devout. With this information, development planners can look at the warnings from the past as well as discover areas where the sacred texts allow development to take place. The success of this venture can only be seen over the very long term, but now a complete sacred development and conservation map of Mongolia can be made. It will be used along with economic models, think-tank studies, and all the other paraphernalia of contemporary development structures to give Mongolia a chance for a sustainable and biologically diverse future.

The president of the World Bank, James Wolfensohn, summed up these ideas:

> The changes in Mongolia since the collapse of Communism ten years ago have shown that the country's religious traditions have formed a firm basis upon which to rebuild a country with a strong historical perspective and identity. This rebuilding must encompass more than just infrastructure; the links between physical and psychological recovery should be addressed as well. This process will involve rebuilding people's memories, hopes and

---

7. O. Sukhbaatar, *Sacred Sites of Mongolia* (Ulaanbaatar: World Wide Fund for Nature/ Alliance of Religion and Conservation, 2002), 24.

beliefs. One way to aid in the process of rebuilding is to document Mongolia's sacred lands, an act which will in turn help to guide the ways in which land and resources are used.[8]

The pagodas of Cambodia

The third example comes from Cambodia, where a small project working with Buddhist monks and a range of government and NGO groups has yielded such good results that it is now being extended to Vietnam and Laos. The project depends on the fact that in all villages and many towns in Cambodia, the center of the community is the pagoda. With the support of some overseas sponsors and advisers as well as local government officials, a local nongovernmental group, Mlup Baitong, has been working with the Buddhist communities. The priorities have been to protect the monastery forests and to open up the pagodas for discussions about environmental issues. The 14 pagodas in the main project have 360 monks and 34 nuns—but they reach out to more than 13,000 villagers.

First Mlup Baitong helped organize workshops for monks and nuns, who were later inspired to talk to the villagers about how to preserve the natural environment. So after 55 workshops for the monks, there were 450 village lectures, and several discussions about nature held on closed-circuit radio on Buddhist holy days. So far nine pagodas have conducted water surveys to document their wells and ponds, calculate their total usage of water, and measure contamination—following which they have dug new wells, introduced rainwater jars and water filters, and installed latrines. Two pagodas have been involved in building improved cooking stoves. When it was shown that these burn half as much wood as ordinary stoves, Mlup Baitong started a campaign throughout the region to provide them to all pagodas.

Monks have also been involved in building tree nurseries and planting seedlings, with eight schools adopting nurseries and compost bins as part of a school environment program. So far more than 1,000 trees have been planted—ritually marked together with seedling ordination ceremonies. In its small but effective way, this project has produced a model that works. And because it draws upon the basis of Buddhism and its relationship to local communities as well as national governments, it can be replicated across the Buddhist world.

ARC and the World Bank are helping Buddhists create an Asian Buddhist Network, to enable Buddhists across the continent to exchange experiences about development projects and conservation. This network is not just for the monasteries: it is also bringing together political, eco-

---

8. Sukhbaatar, *Sacred Sites of Mongolia*, 5.

nomic, and social leaders who are actively Buddhist or whose countries are predominantly Buddhist.

The biodiversity of beliefs

All these examples share a celebration of diversity; they are not an attempt to get everyone to think in the same way. In 1986, when Prince Philip invited five major faiths and representatives of the environmental movement to Assisi to explore how they could become partners in conservation, it quickly became clear that there was a problem. Of course there were many common concerns shared by the groups, but what was to be made of their differences? They had very different conservation, environmental, ecological, and scientific ideas—indeed they couldn't even agree on terminology. In the end everyone decided to adopt a very simple slogan, which is still the basis for such work, alliances, and cooperation between faith and secular groups today.

The slogan was: "Come, proud of what you bring of your own, but humble enough to listen." In many ways this (rather than the common denominator, as some would like it) is the basic creed of pluralism. So often in so-called interfaith work, differences are glossed over in the name of a superficial unity, which benefits no one. The religions do what they do not because of some general belief in the Divine, but because of very specific beliefs.

In Papua New Guinea, for example, the Evangelical Alliance has developed a training center for Christian pastors and laity to learn forest management, biodiversity, and general ecological awareness. The center itself is an extraordinary place, deep in the forest where training and worship can take place within the very environment that the participants want to protect. But the heart of the project is not the training center but the Bible, which the Christians of Papua New Guinea consider to be their natural source of authority. They believe that the Bible contains the true Word of God, revealed in order that humanity may live a more godly life, saved by Christ and redeemed in order to redeem the world.

This kind of language—focused on Christ, God, and the Bible—might alienate many in the secular world, but in Papua New Guinea, where 97 percent of people are Christian, it makes much more sense than statistical studies and the application of international strategies for the protection of biodiversity. These Christians are rereading and reinterpreting the Bible in light of the threats to the biodiversity of their country and its precious forests. Were the Bible not placed at the center of the project, the Churches would have no real sense of involvement, and one of the main networks—respected, owned, and adhered to by the vast majority of people in the country—would have been left out.

The World Bank recently hosted a meeting of conservative evangelical leaders organized by A Rocha, a Christian NGO, and chaired by the Bishop of Liverpool. It focused on discussing the biblical basis for caring for creation and considering the place of environmental issues among this opinion-forming group. The group is significant both within the United States and in many of the Bank's client countries, and yet it could be typified as being at worst negative or at best neutral when it comes to environmental stewardship; they spend much time debating and defending creation but virtually no time caring for it.

Both these projects are pluralist, in that a Bible worldview is working hand in hand with other worldviews (represented by the World Bank, ARC, and other groups) and everyone agrees that preserving what Christians would call God's creation, and environmentalists would call biodiversity, is vitally important. The Papua New Guinea project is working because all the partners realize they are speaking different languages, but ultimately they all believe in a similar goal.

Some people, who fear difference and diversity, have a rigid vision of the future. For them the perfect future involves one world, united by one belief (be that, for example, Christianity, Baha'ism, democracy, or Marxism) and united in one goal (of peace, sustainability, or whatever). All it needs, they think, is one more missionary push, five-year plan, or big funding effort, and the rest of the world will begin to think as they do. But this is never going to happen, and it never *should* happen. There is no record of any one belief system totally dominating the world. And human beings are far too awkward for that ever to happen in the future.

Appropriately, one of the best models for how human beings can conserve nature comes from nature itself. One of the key arguments for protecting biodiversity is that without it, evolution cannot continue and life on earth could die out. All around us there are millions of species: some are dying out, some are just emerging, some are irrelevant to evolution, some are possibly crucial. The earth needs this range for those times of vast extinction, with the dominant species dying out and leaving space for others.

So if diversity of species is fundamental to physical evolution, then perhaps diversity of thoughts, beliefs, values, and ways of life is also fundamental. And those people who believe that evolution and creation are the work of God might like to see this diversity of thought as part of the Purpose of God—the very weft and warp of life itself. This pluralism is one of the best models for tackling those complicated conservation problems for which no one system can offer a sure way forward; it is as important for effective faith-based investment as it is for grassroots projects that involve participants from different backgrounds. And as I will explore in the final chapter, perhaps one of the greatest ways to invest in nature's future is not only to accept differences and diversity, but also to celebrate them.

5

Celebrating the Environment

God called to Moses out of the burning bush. "Moses, Moses!" And he said,
"Here I am." Then He said, "Come no closer! Remove the sandals from
your feet, for the place on which you stand is holy ground."
—Hebrew Bible, Book of Exodus, The Torah (3: 4-5)

The intention is to introduce you to reality, not to imitate nature.
It is to show you not what you see, but what is real. . . .
Everything in Creation—including humanity—was created pure but not
perfect, and the purpose of being born is to reach your true potential.
—Brother Aidan, icon painter

Religion, like every other human organization, fails. It fails to achieve most of its own self-proclaimed goals, and it fails to prevent abuse and exploitation of its structures, powers, and beliefs. In this it is no different from every other human organization.

Yet religion, as we have observed before, survives and has survived longer than any empire, monarchy, nation, or company. Somewhere along the line the main faiths have discovered a few basic truths about how the world and humanity behave and why—and this has been the core of their success. And they succeed often enough to be worth perpetuating.

The secrets to success

What are the secrets of this ability to survive, indeed even to grow? One of them is that religions tend to provide what people tend to need. At their best, they can give meaning as much to the ordinary as to the extraordinary; can provide comfort as well as challenges; can stimulate as well as create places for rest; can offer entire cosmologies to explain the meaning of life, as well as provide a quick prayer to get someone through the worries of an exam or an argument. In popular language they offer a holistic view of life that few other groups can get close to offering.

This was better understood a hundred years ago than it is today. In Britain, Germany, Italy, Russia, and Mexico, for example, the emerging socialist movements both admired and feared the power of the Church. They set out deliberately to counter its influence by creating alternative belief systems, in effect new "Churches," which they housed in special buildings called "labor churches" or "halls of science." There the energies, skills, music, Sunday schools, teachings, liturgies, and even the annual cycle of festivals usually found in Churches were replicated, but with a socialist content. They wanted socialism to became a new faith. They all failed. The fact is that humanity does not live by bread alone—nor by ideals. Each of us spins a web of stories, legends, and beliefs around ourselves and those we love, and these stories are part of what makes life possible.

The importance of telling tales

As I showed in chapter 3, all religions pass on their messages and their ethos by telling stories. Here I want to show *how* this skill can be extended to pass on messages about the environment and social development.

Just for a moment, think about how you tell your own story. From the tens of thousands of events in your life, you will probably have selected no more than four or five which, if someone asks you who you are or why you do what you do, you will tell by way of explanation. Even statements as simple as "I am married" or "I am a mother" or "I work for X company" or "I had a tough childhood" are stories spun to help make sense of a vast and vague world and to provide the questioner with an acceptable answer. You will have stories about your relationships with your parents and partners, about what kind of people your children or your friends are, about your beliefs, and about the hardships you have suffered and how you dealt with them. And you will also have stories that you don't want to tell other people, but that you tell yourself.

The fact that you are reading this book probably means that you care about the issues of conservation or faith or both. If someone was interviewing you and said, "Tell me what person or what experience led you to this interest," what would you say? In my own work, for example, because I am officially "religious," people tend to tell me why they do things, not just how they do them. It is one of the many enjoyable parts of running an alliance between religions and conservation—indeed I often think it is what makes it possible. But all that I do is provide an excuse for something that just about everyone would like to talk about. Could your organization also create such a space for drawing out the personal in order to understand the professional? Is there space there for stories?

Beneath the professional jargon, CVs, profiles, and so on lies a real truth. It was not facts and figures that persuaded us to get involved: it was for reasons more personal, complex, and varied—reasons that are best explained by stories. Given that we interpret the world through stories even if we sometimes like to call them facts, it is somewhat surprising that in the environmental and development movements people rarely use stories but rely instead on dry statistics or facts with no context. This can lead us to miss the point of an activity and at its worst can even bring us to destroy the very thing we seek to understand.

An extreme example of this is given by the writer and environmentalist storyteller Thomas Pakenham in *Remarkable Trees of the World*.[1] He tells of a university researcher in Utah who wanted to confirm that a certain tree was the oldest in the world. So he obtained permission from the National Park Service authorities to use a special drill to remove a central core from the tree so he could count the rings. Unfortunately the drill broke. The researcher, anxious to retrieve the precious drill, was then given permission to have the tree cut down. After it was felled, the researcher retrieved his drill and learned he had been right. The tree was more than 4,900 years old and was perhaps the oldest living thing on the planet—or rather it had been.

But what good did it do him to know this? The point is, the researcher wanted a story, and he didn't realize that for it to be true he didn't necessarily need Guinness Book of Records facts. Perhaps if the researcher had talked to local people they might have told him ancient tales about this ancient tree and he could have let it live, with uncounted rings, for another thousand years.

Yet stories can help people change their behavior: indeed our Utah researcher unwittingly provided such a behavior-changing story by being an example of what most people do not want to be. And here we can learn from the great religions. For it is by telling and remembering traditional stories that the religions are often most persuasive and positive in protecting the environment, both by reminding people of the right way of doing things and by promoting a greater sense of responsibility for natural resources. Here are two stories that show the importance—and the possibilities—of storytelling.

---

1. Thomas Pakenham, *Remarkable Trees of the World* (New York: W. W. Norton, 2002).

Muhammad and the river

One day, according to the Hadith (a book of traditional and authenticated accounts of the words and actions of the Prophet Muhammad), the Prophet was traveling from one town to the next with his followers. They were just crossing a river when it became time for prayers. Naturally they used the river to perform the ritual ablutions required before prayer. However, the followers of the Prophet were astonished to see him enter the river with a little bowl. This he filled with water and it was this water with which he performed the ablutions. When asked why, surrounded by a whole river, he took so little water to use, he said that just because there is plenty this does not give us the right to waste or to take more than we really need.[2]

This is one of the most powerful stories that Muslims use to teach about our need to respect the environment. And even today, in the modern world, when Islamic teachers and leaders need to remind people not to waste resources this is one of the main examples they will use. Sometimes when faith-based environmentalists work on projects, all they need to do is remind local people of the stories they know already.

Krishna and the serpent

Similarly, in India, a story of Lord Krishna and the evil serpent has helped develop river environment schemes (and give local people a renewed sense of responsibility for that environment) in ways that statistics could not begin to do.

The ancient legend tells that once upon a time, an evil serpent lived in the sacred Yamuna River that flows across the center of India and into the Ganges. The serpent's foul breath blasted the crops growing along the river and its polluting body fouled the water, injuring all life. The people started to weep and the creatures of the river started to cry out, and eventually their distress reached the ears of the Lord Krishna. He sped to the river and—after a dramatic three-day battle—killed the serpent and freed the waters and the people from its evil influence.

In the 1990s it became evident that the Yamuna was reaching dangerous levels of pollution. Hindu communities were able to draw upon this legend and use it to awaken local awareness of the problem. They stated that the pollution was the return of the evil serpent in a new and more

---

2. *Ibn Maja, Sunan Ibn Maja,* ed. F. 'Abd al-Baqi (Turkey, 1972), 1, 146. This Muslim story is echoed in the Hindu saying: "Everything animate or inanimate that is within the universe is controlled and owned by the Lord. One should therefore accept only those things necessary for himself, which are set aside as his quota, and one should not accept other things, knowing well to whom they belong." From *Sri Isopanshad,* Mantra 1.

ugly form. Today, they said, Krishna needs human beings to be his hands in the battle against the serpent—and it is humans who must work together to eliminate pollution in the sacred river. Once again, it is the specific Krishna nature of the story and the insight into tackling this very real environmental issue that has made this possible.

The importance of images and beauty

Another skill—secret if you like—of the great religions is their understanding of the role of art. They see it as a necessity, not as a luxury, and as a way of explaining ideas and roles that cannot be explained in words. Every great faith uses art not only to explain itself but also to explain glory. Even Islam, which forbids the depiction of any living creature (including angels and of course God) on the grounds that it constitutes idolatry, has inspired the most exquisite architecture, architecture that—by using geometry as a sacred art form—is a symbol of unity.

To create and treasure something lovely, something that has drawn upon the best craftspeople, the finest materials, and the most loving attention, is a testimony to that which the human spirit can achieve. This is why it is so problematic that recently, and particularly in the West, a variety of lowest-level utilitarianism has taken hold in many groups that design structures for the poor and dispossessed. Why should these people not have places and experiences of beauty? Indeed, perhaps they are the ones who need them most.

Here is a powerful story about beauty, heard from a Christian aid worker based in Bangladesh. He knew of a family living outside Dhaka whose village had been badly hit by floods. They had absolutely nothing left and several of the five children were sick. The father was given emergency money by an international charity, but a day later charity workers were horrified to see him and his entire family emerging from a matinee showing at the local cinema. They challenged him and asked him why he didn't spend their money on food, clothes, or some other "necessity"—why he had wasted it. The man replied that he knew his family would never have enough to eat or wear and would be struggling for the rest of their lives. But for one glorious afternoon they had been able to let all of that go and enjoy the sight of romance and color and escapism and adventure. That, he said, would feed their spirits when their bodies were hungry.

The great religions realized a long time ago that beauty is not a luxury but a necessary celebration of both humanity and the Divine. This is why when reforming groups (who insist on a puritanical and legalistic reading of their traditions) rise up, they first tend to target things of beauty. This is because these things bear testimony to a world vision from their faith that is too wide for the purist and too exciting for the legalist.

Yet this vision of beauty in faith is one that many groups are begin-ning to appreciate. For example, for some years the Swiss Agency for Development and Cooperation (SDC) has been a sponsor of Art for the World. The agency's director, Walter Fust, explains:

> Over the past five years, the Swiss Agency for Development and Cooper-ation has sponsored a series of three exhibitions by Art for the World. That may surprise some people and prompt them to ask: Isn't Swiss develop-ment cooperation intended to meet the urgent basic needs of poverty-stricken people? For example, isn't clean drinking water more important than painting and sculpting?
> The questions are justified. Our partners in the South would reply that [humanity], as everyone knows, does not live by bread alone. As a wide-ranging study by the World Bank has shown, culture, even for people liv-ing in extreme poverty, is no luxury. In fact, in many respects it is central to their lives.
> What impresses me about Art for the World is how it has succeeded in mastering the skill in balancing between contemporary and sometimes elitist art and social engagement. For years, Art for the World has repre-sented values which are also important for the SDC: dialogue between cul-tures, tolerance and a spirit of solidarity.[3]

In the rather puritanical world of many development agencies that (unlike the SDC) seek to make the world better only on their terms, the notions of beauty, storytelling, and fun don't have much of a look-in. Yet working with such forces can be exciting, constructive, and ultimately effective. If we do not remember that our world is beautiful as well as functional, why should we care enough to save those parts of it that are not immediately useful to us?

I want to look at two examples of faiths that have expressed the essence of their beliefs through art. The first is Orthodox Christianity, which has a powerful explanation of the role of iconography.

An Orthodox icon

The Orthodox model assumes that each aspect of creation—the heavens, the rocks, the wilderness, the stars, and humanity in its diverse forms and beliefs—has its role to play in caring for the Creator. This is power-fully summed up in the Vespers hymn that is sung on the evening of Christmas Day, with its description of the Virgin Mary giving birth to Christ in a cave. The hymn follows the Orthodox version of the Nativ-

---

3. *Art for the World* (Geneva: Art for the World, 2001), 15.

ity,[4] with all the elements of the natural and human world giving offerings to God in his incarnation as a vulnerable child:

What shall we offer Thee, O Christ,
who for our sake was seen on earth as man?
For every thing created by Thee offers Thee thanks.
The angels offer Thee their hymns;
the heavens, the star;
the Magi, their gifts;
the shepherds, their wonder;
the earth, the cave;
the wilderness, the manger;
while we offer Thee a Virgin Mother,
O pre-eternal God, have mercy upon us . . .

It is a model of diversity that the Orthodox Church has now explicitly extended to the role that all of us have in protecting life on earth, each offering our own (different) strengths and abilities. Politicians, economists, scientists, clergy, leaders, journalists, students, workers, parents: each of us has a distinct role that no one else can play in quite the same way.

Since the mid-1990s Bartholomew I, the Ecumenical Patriarch of Constantinople (who is First Among Equals of all the patriarchs of Orthodox Churches around the world), has organized an extraordinary series of floating seminars on conservation, based on exactly this model. These unprecedented meetings—held on the great seas and rivers that surround the traditional heartlands of Orthodoxy, including the Black Sea, the Aegean, and the Danube—have brought together political leaders, scientists, the media, religious leaders, economists, and others to talk about major issues like water pollution. Together these men and women have discussed, planned, thought, reflected, lectured, and prayed, in what for many participants has been a revealing and life-changing experience of partnership and celebration of diversity.

It is a vision of our place and role in nature, which encompasses rather than seeks to control, and which does not only accept but actively welcomes pluralism rather than trying to make everyone think the same way. This model is encapsulated in Orthodox icon paintings, which are physical embodiments of the Church's teaching that it is only through material things that God's beauty can be appreciated (see Figure 1).[5] As

---

4. According to the nonbiblical second-century text "The Book of James," Mary and Joseph were some eight miles outside Bethlehem when Mary realized she was about to give birth. Putting her in a cave in a mountain, Joseph hurried on to Bethlehem to find a midwife. When he returned he found Jesus had already been born.

5. "I shall not cease reverencing matter, by means of which my salvation has been achieved . . ." (St. John of Damascus, *On Holy Images,* 1.16).

Figure 1.   Christian icon: Saint Charalampuf

Late 19th-century icon of Saint Charalampuf illustrating scenes from his life and witnessed by God and Christ, who break into the icon from the top left.

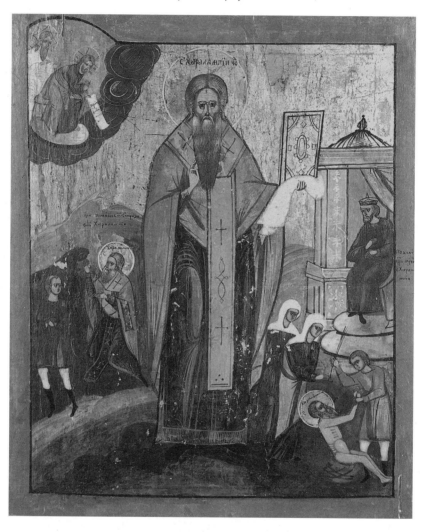

the U.K.-based icon painter Brother Aidan explains: "The intention is to introduce you to reality, not to imitate nature. It is to show you not what you see, but what is real."

So the figures of saints often go beyond the frame to show how there are no real boundaries, and buildings tend to have a strange perspective—you can see left and right and up and down, which is meant to represent the way God "sees" the whole world at once. Taking natural pigments like ochre and lapis lazuli and malachite and beautifying them by using them in art is a simple expression of the Orthodox teaching that creation—including humanity—was created pure but not perfect and the purpose of being born is to reach your true potential.[6]

Icons make a powerful model by which the conservation movement, with all the richness and diversity of its input and membership, can view itself. Imagine putting together a partnership of diverse groups, interests, and beliefs, as if you were creating an icon—an icon that offers everyone the chance to be more by working together than they can be by themselves. It is a challenging but also an achievable image.

A Buddhist mandala

Another way of using religious art to help us think about partnership and pluralism is to look at a Buddhist mandala (see Figure 2). These paintings are models of reality based upon Buddhist insights into the human mind. They draw you in, layer upon layer, from the outside of the painting, which represents where we stand now, toward the Buddha-nature (reality if you like) at the center of the painting.

On the way you travel across different worlds and layers of meaning, from the sensual through the reflective to the extraordinary emptiness at the center. On this journey, you are asked to encounter the diverse levels of meaning, existence, purpose, and intention that surround us all—and which we so rarely stop to explore. They are like layers of skin wrapped so tightly around us that we cannot see them. The mandala takes us pictorially and psychologically into an exploration of these, peeling the layers off until we come to the heart of things.

The icon and the mandala have provided two of the greatest cultures of the world with the means to make sense of the seen and the unseen worlds. Although throughout the world (starting, arguably, with the West) we are forgetting how to see things symbolically, for many people these kinds of models are better and more helpful images than pie charts or diagrams of organizational structures.

In the past there has been a problem when stories and visions of what is beautiful or right have clashed. Religion has often been at the forefront of such conflicts because many of the faiths assume that their vision is the only true one, or at the least, the only appropriate one for their people and their lands. The point here is that all of us—whether we call ourselves religious or secular—need to see the world differently.

---

6. Victoria Finlay, *Colour: Travels through the Paintbox* (London: Sceptre, 2002), 25–26.

Figure 2. Tibetan mandala: Medicinal plants

The viewer is drawn into the heart of the mandala where the Buddha resides. The outer layers, representing the sensual world, are made up of medicinal plants.

At present we see only fragments and because we tend to defend the vision of our fragment as the truth, we find it hard to relate to other people's visions.

Quiet and special places

Another "secret" of the great religions is their ability to provide quiet places—or at least special places—in the communities that observe them.

Think of a Shinto garden, a village churchyard, a lofty mosque, a neighborhood synagogue, or a Buddhist temple. Many religions have traditions of "sanctuary" in these quiet places, and many of the most successful religion and conservation projects are ones that recognize the power of these places and extend it.

These include, for example, the Living Churchyards project mentioned in chapter 3, in which more than 6,000 English churches developed management plans for their graveyards that allowed nature to flourish. By not cutting the grass often, by leaving monuments to crumble naturally, and by providing facilities like bat boxes, nesting boxes, and even wetlands, the churches created wonderful habitats for a range of wild species. Some of these living churchyards have displays showing the increase in the number of species as a result of these policies. Here the local communities, including many people who are not churchgoers, can make a difference. Many churches have church primary schools, and these often play a crucial role in working with the churchyards and educating not only the pupils but their parents as well in the importance of sanctuary for a wildlife that is increasingly under threat.

In Yunnan Province in southwest China there is a lake called Dianchi, which conservationists have labeled a "hotspot" of freshwater biodiversity. In the 1950s it was recorded as having 24 indigenous fish species, at least 11 of which were endemic, as well as dozens of endemic crustacean and mollusk species. However, since that time these have been under threat—partly because the water quality has been declining with dangerously high levels of phosphorus and nitrogen, partly because of competition from the 30 or so introduced species of fish, and partly because of the threats from corresponding new diseases and parasites. By 1994 there were possibly only seven endemic and five other indigenous fish species left.

The decline could have been even worse, had it not been for the local Buddhist temples. Four of the rarest endemic fish species[7] have probably only survived because of the unconscious sanctuary that the temples have offered. The sacred springs near these temples—with powerful names like Black Dragon Pool, Blue Dragon Pool, and Dragon Pond—have been kept clean, with fishing forbidden. And it is here that these rare species continue to live. The temples have in effect practiced a sort of passive conservation for centuries, thus enabling the survival of the species through protection of their habitat.

In the past few years, provincial, state, and international governments have set up the Yunnan Environment Project in conjunction with the

---

7. *Sinocyclocheilus grahami grahami, Schizothorax grahami, Discogobio yunnanensis,* and *Yunnanilus pleurotaenia.*

World Bank,[8] various international agencies including ARC, and most importantly the local office of the Buddhist Association of China. The Buddhists' role as the historic but passive guardians of the lake has now been recognized. But more than that, now that the Buddhists have themselves recognized what they have done, they have been able to turn their passive protection into an active program of protection and education. And the springs that in some cases are the only known sites for some species are now actively valued.

This is an example of the inherent role of religious sites in China, where partnerships with secular agencies are able to develop in ways that the Buddhists themselves would not necessarily have considered. The Buddhist Association of China elsewhere in China has proved to be very responsive to the conservation message.

Missionaries and pilgrims

Many secular organizations—including the World Bank, WWF, and the United Nations—talk about their staff going "on mission" or explain their policies in "mission statements." This is nothing new. But in doing so, these organizations may be perpetuating one of the greatest mistakes of the religions, one that the faiths themselves have tried to change. Virtually all the founders of the major religions spoke about the spiritual life as being a journey or a pilgrimage. This model has shaped the major faiths, and pilgrimage is central to every single world religion. Think of the Hajj in Islam, which every able-bodied Muslim should undertake at least once in his or her life. By insisting that everyone dress the same and walk together, the Hajj emphasizes everyone's equal standing before God. Or consider Christianity, with its ancient centers of pilgrimage. The Church made every country sacred so you did not have to go to Jerusalem; you could go, for example, to Santiago de Compostela, Canterbury, or the great Mexican shrine of Our Lady of Guadalupe.

Many religions forgot this tradition of traveling humbly and have launched great missions whose hallmark has been an intense desire to change the lives of those whom they missionize. But this model has increasingly been rejected by the major faiths in favor of a return to the encounter of travelers, pilgrims, and personal witnesses to the power of religion.

---

8. The project is taking advantage of a major World Bank–financed project that has been serving to improve water quality conditions in the lake, and applying a biodiversity dimension to its infrastructure, policy, and regulatory measures by restoring natural habitats and other activities that will conserve as many as possible of the highly range-restricted endemic species.

What if the new missionary movements of the secular world—the environmental movement, the development community, and international agencies—talked of pilgrimage rather than of mission? What if their staff thought of walking humbly to other countries and relying upon the traditions of hospitality just as pilgrims do? What a psychological difference that would make and what a role model for the people in those countries.

In its Sacred Land Program ARC has drawn together from the experiences of all the major faiths seven separate stages of pilgrimage. These are ideas, not rules, and explore how any journey can become a pilgrimage.

The first stage involves thinking about being a pilgrim rather than just traveling from A to B. The second is about recognizing that journeys are entities in themselves and they can—if you allow them—take on a life of their own. They are not just a means to an end. The third stage of pilgrimage is becoming aware of the people with whom you are traveling and of why you are together, discovering what each of you brings as well as being honest about some of the tensions. The fourth is about understanding the story that has brought you there: your story. In the fifth stage you lose your role as an observer and become part of the landscape and part of somebody else's story.

The sixth stage is to actually look at what you are passing through, and the seventh and final stage is to recognize that at the end of the journey you should be different from the person who set out. If every business meeting, every overseas trip, and every project were to use these ideas, they would be so much more effective and enjoyable.

Cycles and celebrations

Ramadan/Eid, Lent/Easter, Pansa/Wesak, Rosh Hashanah/Yom Kippur, Ashwin/Divali . . .[9] Every religion has cycles of reflection followed by celebration: fasts are followed by feasts. The major faiths have all structured annual cycles that help carry people through the year, making the monotony of everyday life manageable and celebrating the changes of the natural seasons. They know that you cannot make people repent, fast, or reflect the whole time. You have to let them have a good time as well—or what is the point?

This has proved to be one of the most important insights that the faiths are offering to the secular world as well as to their own followers. Many NGOs, agencies, and other worthy groups present a consistently

---

9. See Glossary.

gloomy picture of the world in the hope that shock tactics will produce compassion or repentance. They usually don't. We are now confronted with the phenomenon of "compassion fatigue." The faiths also have tough things to say about being human and the shortcomings and short-falls of human society. They call for repentance, conversion, salvation, and liberation from the elements of human behavior that are destructive. But they also know how to have a good time.

Unless you can offer a vision of the wonder of living, why should any-body bother to change? Around the world the religious involvement in environmental and development work has found a special role for this understanding of how and why humans find motivation: celebrations of what is good, encouraging, and exciting in the way the world is devel-oping have proved enormously popular. Not just with the religious com-munities but with the wider public.

For example, the Environmental Sabbath in the United States is a weekend-long Muslim-Jewish-Christian (and increasingly Sikh-Hindu-Buddhist) celebration through prayer, music, action, sermons, drama, and silence. It rejoices in the achievements of the past year and sets out the challenges for the year to come. As a result of the public commitment to ecology by the present Ecumenical Patriarch and the leadership he has given to the other Orthodox Church leaders, September 1 has since 1993 been a day of prayer and action in every Orthodox Christian community worldwide, with special services, hymns, and music.

The month-long fast of Ramadan has for centuries been a time when Muslims reflect on their relationship to God and their reliance on His bounty. It was therefore a natural time of the year to develop an explicit environmental message that drew out for the contemporary world the significance of this ancient time of reflection. In Indonesia, as part of a World Bank and ARC joint project, Muslim scholars and community leaders are developing a series of meditations for each day of Ramadan, weaving contemporary environmental information with traditional Islamic texts, and suggesting specific actions to help preserve the envi-ronment. At the end of Ramadan comes the glorious festival of Eid where the wonders and bounty of God are celebrated. What more appropriate end to a time of environmental reflection?

New ideologies have always understood the power of festivals but have rarely succeeded in tapping it effectively. In the late eighteenth cen-tury the French revolution created a whole new calendar of secular fes-tivals. Neither the calendar nor the occasions lasted more than 10 years. In the late 1980s various environmental groups attempted to establish annual Earth Days, but these have not been fully accepted, partly because they don't particularly mean anything.

For a festival to succeed it needs to be grafted onto something deeper, with a period of preparation leading to the celebration. The remarkable thing about festivals is that they can be traced back in time. Easter, for example, builds upon the tradition of celebrating the coming of spring and new life, a tradition that predates Christianity by thousands of years—and indeed the word "Easter" refers to the deity Eostre whose rebirth was celebrated in ancient Celtic rituals.

An interesting story about these problems is that of the millennium celebrations in Britain. Two very different projects reflected different worlds and values in a most telling way.

At a government level, the year 2000 was marked by the creation of a giant dome at the Greenwich meridian containing a series of supposedly popular exhibitions on the themes of time, history, and the future. It was a disaster. The costs were huge—nearly £1 billion, which could have built five new hospitals, and of which only around £120 million were recouped. The expected crowds never materialized and the ephemeral nature of this supposed monument to 2,000 years is an all too powerful example of the transient nature of contemporary culture.

At the other end of the scale is perhaps one of the most successful British millennium projects—and one that should still be visible at the turn of the next millennium. In 1999 the U.K. Conservation Foundation came up with the idea of taking cuttings from yew trees that were alive at the time of Christ (whose birth provided the reason after all for there being a millennium celebration). There are several hundred of these trees scattered across Britain, almost all within the sacred confines of churchyards. It was hoped that several hundred churches would take up the gift of a yew sapling to commemorate the millennium. But in the end more than 8,000 saplings were distributed to as many churches, and huge crowds, way beyond expectation, packed cathedrals and local churches for the blessing of these tiny plants. In a thousand years' time, one in 20 of these yews could well be still alive. And in the next hundred years the majority of these trees will provide shelter and habitat for species in churchyards, and act as a memorial to the local enthusiasm for both nature and the sacred, which was such a hallmark of this splendid project.

The discarded husk of the Millennium Dome and the thousands of new yew trees across the face of Britain illustrate the difference between putting on a show that a government decided was good for the people and creating a story that others can share. One was a project literally without roots that was afraid to be honest about the reason for the celebration—the birth of Christ. The other chose one of the most powerful sacred trees of ancient Britain—and said let's celebrate through it.

I return to the image that began the book—of a messenger rushing in sweaty and full of amazing, terrifying news that the end of the world is nigh, and of a tranquil gardener listening carefully, but getting on with planting a sapling before going to find out the truth. In a way the international agencies, environmental lobby groups, and governments, with their various 3-, 5-, or 10-year plans, are the messengers. The insight of the faiths is that although these messengers might be speaking the truth, it is in the end probably more useful to finish planting the tree first.

Because even when everything seems to be crumbling we have to believe that life on earth will go on. And we have to help make it happen.

Part 2
The Faith Statements on Ecology

6

Introduction

In 1986 the World Wide Fund for Nature (WWF) International invited five religions to meet with the key environmental organizations in Assisi, Italy. The faiths were asked to do two things. First, they were asked to look at what environmental projects they had running at the time. There were very few. Second, they were asked to produce, prior to the Assisi meeting, their own statements on ecology. These five original statements proved to be a catalyst for a real participation of the faiths in ecology. Each faith was asked to write as simply and clearly as possible and to take no more than 2,000 words to describe from their scriptures, teachings, and traditions, their views on caring for nature. These statements opened a window into the beliefs, into the very soul of each faith. They provided the environmental world with arguments from within each tradition as to why the faith should now do more to ensure the protection of nature. The statements also stirred debate and study within each faith, for we asked that, where possible, major institutions within each faith, rather than individuals, prepare the statements. Thus for Islam, it was the Muslim World League; for Judaism, the World Jewish Congress; and for Christianity, the Franciscan Orders. In the case of both Buddhism and Hinduism, there was no clear major body that could speak for the majority of the faithful. Therefore we worked with the Dalai Lama on Buddhism and with leading scholars such as Dr. Karan Singh, former minister of the environment in the Indian government and a leading Hindu thinker, for Hinduism.

By 1995, when ARC was launched, the original five had grown to nine. The Baha'is, Daoists, Jains, and Sikhs had created their own statements. In the case of the Jains, the need to create a document reflecting the views of all three main traditions in Jainism spurred the three groups to enter into discussion for the first time in many centuries, and led ultimately to the creation of an Institute of Jainology which now brings the three traditions together on all sorts of issues. The Baha'is have a very clear structure of authority that embraces all Baha'i communities, and it was through the Baha'i International Community that their statement was issued. For the Sikhs, once again, there was no clear body with which to work at that time, and so such a body was created by Sikh scholars in the United Kingdom.

The original Assisi Statements, as they came to be known, have been reprinted worldwide in forums as diverse as the websites of each faith; United Nations publications such as *Cultural and Spiritual Values of Biodiversity;* religious education books produced for state schools in the United Kingdom; many other books such as the WWF India special edition and *World Religions and the Environment* by Professor O. P. Dwivedi of India; and the Environmental Sabbath materials produced in the United States. Perhaps more importantly, they have appeared in translation, in languages relevant to each faith, and have been distributed through faith publishing networks.

In 1995 we asked all the faiths to revisit their original statements and to amend, enlarge, or consolidate the insights in the light of their new experiences. These revised faith statements are the ones published here, along with the two new statements for the Shinto and Zoroastrians, who joined ARC in 2000 at the Kathmandu WWF/ARC Sacred Gifts Celebration.

The statements are fascinating for a number of reasons. First, they open up the teachings and insights of each faith in a unique way. They were written not by scholars who just study the particular faith, but rather by people who actually believe in the faith traditions of which they write. In most cases, the statements are the product of the major bodies within each faith. Thus, for example, the Christian one built upon the original Franciscan (Catholic) statement and drew in contributions from the World Council of Churches, the largest organization representing the non-Catholic Churches, as well as from the Orthodox Churches, the largest Christian faith group after the Catholics.

Second, the style and structure of each statement reflect something of the approach and attitude of the faith to both the notion of the written word and the notion of what is central to that faith. Some of the statements are quite short; for example, the Jain statement is succinct because the emphasis in Jainism is on action and on the central tenet of ahimsa, nonviolence. That is so fundamental that all else is commentary. Meanwhile, Judaism and Sikhism, both faiths with a strong tradition of the written word as a manifestation of the Divine, explore the consequences of the insights contained in different texts within their holy scriptures. Each statement is a mini-adventure into the mind and worldview of each faith. This is why they are so diverse, different, and interesting.

These statements, some of them written originally in languages other than English, have been edited for consistency in format and ease of reading. They are copyright-free, as we and the faiths wish them to be printed, broadcast, e-mailed, or otherwise transmitted as often as possible. All we ask is that they be credited to the original source. But in the end, no one owns the wisdom within these faiths and their statements, any more than anyone owns creation itself.

7
Baha'i Faith

This statement was issued by the Baha'i Office of the Environment on behalf of the Baha'i International Community.

In this age of transition toward a world society, protection of the environment and conservation of the earth's resources represent an enormously complex challenge. The rapid progress in science and technology that has united the world physically has also greatly accelerated destruction of the biological diversity and rich natural heritage with which the planet has been endowed. Material civilization, driven by the dogmas of consumerism and aggressive individualism and disoriented by the weakening of moral standards and spiritual values, has been carried to excess.

Only a comprehensive vision of a global society, supported by universal values and principles, can inspire individuals to take responsibility for the long-term care and protection of the natural environment. Baha'is find such a world-embracing vision and system of values in the teachings of Baha'u'llah, which herald an era of planetary justice, prosperity, and unity.

Baha'i teachings on conservation and sustainable development

Baha'u'llah enjoins His followers to develop a sense of world citizenship and a commitment to stewardship of the earth. His writings are imbued with a deep respect for the natural world and for the interconnectedness of all things. They emphasize that the fruits of God's love and obedience to His commandments are dignity, nobility, and a sense of worth. From these attributes emerge the natural inclination to treat one another with love and compassion, and the willingness to sacrifice for the betterment of society. Baha'u'llah also teaches moderation, a commitment to justice, and detachment from the things of this world—spiritual disciplines, which enable individuals to contribute to the establishment of a prosperous and united world civilization. The broad pattern for such a civilization and the principles on which it should be based are set forth in Baha'u'llah's Revelation, a revelation that offers hope to a dispirited humanity and the promise that it is truly possible both to meet the needs of present and future generations and to build a sound foundation for social and economic development. The inspiration and the vision for this civilization are captured in Baha'u'llah's words: "The earth is but one country, and mankind its citizens."

Among the principles guiding the Baha'i approach to conservation and sustainable development, the following are of particular importance:

- Nature reflects the qualities and attributes of God and should, therefore, be greatly respected and cherished.
- All things are interconnected and flourish according to the law of reciprocity.
- The oneness of humanity is the fundamental spiritual and social truth shaping our age.
- Nature reflects the qualities and attributes of God.

Baha'i scriptures describe nature as an emanation of God's will:

Nature in its essence is the embodiment of My Name, the Maker, the Creator. His manifestations are diversified by varying causes, and in this diversity there are signs for men of discernment. Nature is God's Will and is its expression in and through the contingent world. It is a dispensation of Providence ordained by the Ordainer, the All-Wise.

Understanding nature as a reflection of the majesty and an expression of the purpose of God inspires a deep respect for the natural world:

Whatever I behold I readily discover that it maketh Thee known unto me, and it remindeth me of Thy signs, and of Thy tokens, and of Thy testimonies. By Thy glory! Every time I lift up mine eyes unto Thy heaven, I call to mind Thy highness and Thy loftiness, and Thine incomparable glory and greatness; and every time I turn my gaze to Thine earth, I am made to recognize the evidences of Thy power and the tokens of Thy bounty. And when I behold the sea, I find that it speaketh to me of Thy majesty, and of the potency of Thy might, and of Thy sovereignty and Thy grandeur. And at whatever time I contemplate the mountains, I am led to discover the ensigns of Thy victory and the standards of Thine Omnipotence.

This attitude of respect is further reinforced by copious metaphorical references to the natural world woven throughout the Baha'i scriptures. However, while nature is greatly valued and respected, it is not to be worshipped or adopted.

Rather it is to serve the purpose given by God to the human race: to carry forward an ever-advancing civilization. In this regard, the Baha'i faith promotes a worldview that is neither biocentric nor, strictly speaking, anthropocentric, but rather theocentric, with the Revelations of God at its center. Humankind, as it strives to carry out the Divine Will in this, the physical realm, is thus the trustee or steward of nature.

Responsible stewardship of the natural world logically extends to the humane treatment of animals:

> It is not only their fellow human beings that the beloved of God must treat with mercy and compassion, rather must they show forth the utmost loving-kindness to every living creature.
> Train your children from the earliest days to be infinitely tender and loving to animals.

All things are interconnected and flourish according to the law of reciprocity. The principles of interconnectedness and reciprocity underlie the Baha'i understanding of both the operations of the universe and the responsibilities of humankind.

> For every part of the universe is connected with every other part by ties that are very powerful and admit of no imbalance, nor any slackening whatever. . . .
> Cooperation and reciprocity are essential properties that are inherent in the unified system of the world of existence, and without which the entire creation would be reduced to nothingness.
> Were one to observe with an eye that discovereth the realities of all things, it would become clear that the greatest relationship that bindeth the world of being together lieth in the range of created things themselves, and that cooperation, mutual aid, and reciprocity are essential characteristics in the unified body of the world of being, inasmuch as all created things are closely related together and each is influenced by the other or deriveth benefit there from, either directly or indirectly.

Evolutionary processes are explicitly affirmed in Baha'i scriptures:

> All beings, whether large or small, were created perfect and complete from the first, but their perfections appear in them by degrees. The organization of God is one; the evolution of existence is one; the divine system is one. . . . When you consider this universal system, you see that there is

not one of the beings which at its coming into existence has reached the limit of perfection. No, they gradually grow and develop, and then attain the degree of perfection.

The blessings of biodiversity are also highlighted:

Diversity is the essence of perfection and the cause of the appearance of the bestowals of the Most Glorious Lord. . . . This diversity, this difference is like the naturally created dissimilarity and variety of the limbs and organs of the human body, for each one contributed to the beauty, effi- ciency and perfection of the whole. . . . How unpleasing to the eye if all the flowers and plants, the leaves and blossoms, the fruits, the branches, and the trees of that garden were all of the same shape and color! Diversity of hues, form and shape, enriched and adorned the garden, and heightenth the effect thereof . . .

The spiritual and material planes are interconnected and act upon each other:

We cannot segregate the human heart from the environment outside us and say that once one of these is reformed everything will be improved. Man is organic with the world. His inner life molds the environment and is itself also deeply affected by it. The one acts upon the other and every abiding change in the life of man is the result of these mutual reactions.

Given the fundamental unity of science and religion—the intercon- nectedness of the material and spiritual realms—it is not surprising that scientific pursuits are highly praised:

The faculty of intellectual investigation into the secrets of creation . . . is the most praiseworthy power of man, for through its employment and exer- cise the betterment of the human race is accomplished, the development of the virtues of mankind is made possible . . .

However, the exercise of the faculty of investigation must be guided by spiritual principles, especially moderation and humility:

Any agency whatever, though it be the instrument of mankind's greatest good, is capable of misuse.
      If carried to excess, civilization will prove as prolific a source of evil as it had been of goodness when kept within the restraints of moderation.
      Every man of discernment, while walking upon the earth, feeleth indeed abashed, inasmuch as he is fully aware that the thing which is the source of his prosperity, his wealth, his might, his exaltation, his advance- ment and power is, as ordained by God, the very earth which is trodden

beneath the feet of all men. There can be no doubt that whoever is cog-
nizant of this truth, is cleansed and sanctified from all pride, arrogance,
and vainglory. . . .

In light of the interdependence and reciprocity of all parts of nature,
the evolutionary perfection of all beings, and the importance of diversity
"to the beauty, efficiency and perfection of the whole," it is dear to Baha'is
that, in the ordering of human affairs, every effort should be made to
preserve as much as possible the earth's biodiversity and natural order.

Nevertheless, in the process of extending social and economic justice
to the entire human family, certain difficult and possibly irreversible
decisions may have to be taken. Such decisions, Baha'is believe, should
be made within a consultative framework, involving those affected and
taking into account the impact of any resulting policies, programs, and
activities on the quality of life of subsequent generations.

For Baha'is, Baha'u'llah's promise that civilization will exist on this
planet for a minimum of 5,000 centuries makes it unconscionable to
ignore the long-term impact of decisions made today. The world community must, therefore, learn to make use of the earth's natural
resources, both renewable and nonrenewable, in a manner that ensures
sustainability into the distant reaches of time. This does not, however,
mean that Baha'is advocate a "hands-off, back to the woods" policy. On
the contrary, the world civilization that Baha'is believe will eventually
emerge will be animated by a deep religious faith and will be one in
which science and technology will serve humanity and help it to live in
harmony with nature.

The oneness of humanity is, for Baha'is, the fundamental spiritual
and social truth shaping our age, and the operating principle and ultimate goal of humankind's collective life on the planet. It is applicable not
only to the individual, but also to the relationships that must bind all the
states and nations as members of one human family:

> The oneness of mankind . . . implies an organic change in the structure of
> present-day society, a change such as the world has not yet experienced. . . .
> It calls for no less than the reconstruction and the demilitarization of the
> whole civilized world—a world organically unified in all the essential
> aspects of its life, its political machinery, its spiritual aspiration, its trade and
> finance, its script and language, and yet infinite in the diversity of the
> national characteristics of its federated units.
>
> It represents the consummation of human evolution . . . and . . . carries
> with it no more and no less than a solemn assertion that attainment to this
> final stage in this stupendous evolution is not only necessary but
> inevitable, that its realization is fast approaching, and that nothing short
> of a power that is born of God can succeed in establishing it.

Baha'i scriptures maintain that adherence to the principle of the oneness of humanity will have a direct and enduring impact on man's spiritual, social, and physical environments. Universal acceptance of this principle will entail a major restructuring of the world's educational, social, agricultural, industrial, economic, legal, and political systems. This restructuring will facilitate the emergence of a sustainable, just, and prosperous world civilization. Ultimately only a spiritually based civilization—in which science and religion work in harmony—will be able to preserve the ecological balance of the earth, foster stability in the human population, and advance both the material and the spiritual well-being of all peoples and nations.

In conclusion

Baha'i scriptures teach that, as trustees of the planet's vast resources and biological diversity, humanity must seek to protect the "heritage [of] future generations"; see in nature a reflection of the divine; approach the earth, the source of material bounties, with humility; temper its actions with moderation; and be guided by the fundamental spiritual truth of our age, the oneness of humanity. The speed and facility with which we establish a sustainable pattern of life will depend, in the final analysis, on the extent to which we are willing to be transformed, through the love of God and obedience to His Laws, into constructive forces in the process of creating an ever-advancing civilization.

8
Buddhism

This statement was prepared by Kevin Fossey, Buddhist educator and representative of Engaged Buddhism in Europe; Somdech Preah Maha Ghosananda, Patriarch of Cambodian Buddhism; His Excellency Sri Kushok Bakula, 20th Reincarnation of the Buddha's Disciple Bakula, head of Ladakhi Buddhism, and initial rebuilder of Mongolian Buddhism; and Venerable Nhem Kim Teng, Patriarch of Vietnamese Buddhism.

All Buddhist teachings and practice come under the heading of Dharma, which means Truth and the path to Truth. The word Dharma also means "phenomena," and in this way we can consider everything to be within the sphere of the teachings. All outer and inner phenomena, the mind and its surrounding environment, are understood to be inseparable and interdependent. In his own lifetime the Buddha came to understand that the notion that one exists as an isolated entity is an illusion. All things are interrelated; we are interconnected and do not have autonomous existence. Buddha said, "This is because that is; this is not because that is not; this is born because that is born; this dies because that dies." The health of the whole is inseparably linked with the health of the parts, and the health of the parts is inseparably linked with the whole. Everything in life arises through causes and conditions.

Many Buddhist monks such as His Holiness the Dalai Lama, Venerable Thich Nhat Hanh, Venerable Kim Teng, and Venerable Phra Phrachak emphasize the natural relationship between deep ecology and Buddhism. According to the Vietnamese monk Venerable Thich Nhat Hanh:

Buddhists believe that the reality of the interconnectedness of human beings, society and Nature will reveal itself more and more to us as we gradually recover—as we gradually cease to be possessed by anxiety, fear, and the dispersion of the mind. Among the three—human beings, society, and Nature—it is us who begin to effect change. But in order to effect change we must recover ourselves, one must be whole. Since this requires the kind of environment favorable to one's healing, one must seek the kind of lifestyle that is free from the destruction of one's humanness. Efforts to change the environment and to change oneself are both necessary. But we know how difficult it is to change the environment if individuals themselves are not in a state of equilibrium.

In order to protect the environment we must protect ourselves. We protect ourselves by opposing selfishness with generosity, ignorance with wisdom, and hatred with loving kindness. Selflessness, mindfulness, compassion, and wisdom are the essence of Buddhism. We train in Buddhist meditation which enables us to be aware of the effects of our actions, including those destructive to our environment. Mindfulness and clear comprehension are at the heart of Buddhist meditation. Peace is realized when we are mindful of each and every step.

In the words of Maha Ghosananda:

When we respect the environment, then nature will be good to us. When our hearts are good, then the sky will be good to us. The trees are like our mother and father, they feed us, nourish us, and provide us with everything; the fruit, leaves, the branches, the trunk. They give us food and satisfy many of our needs. So we spread the Dharma (truth) of protecting ourselves and protecting our environment, which is the Dharma of the Buddha.

When we accept that we are part of a great human family—that every being has the nature of Buddha—then we will sit, talk, make peace. I pray that this realization will spread throughout our troubled world and bring humankind and the earth to its fullest flowering. I pray that all of us will realize peace in this lifetime and save all beings from suffering.

The suffering of the world has been deep. From this suffering comes great compassion. Great compassion makes a peaceful heart. A peaceful heart makes a peaceful person. A peaceful person makes a peaceful family. A peaceful family makes a peaceful community. A peaceful community makes a peaceful nation. A peaceful nation makes a peaceful world. May all beings live in happiness and peace.

Buddhism as an ecological religion or a religious ecology

The relationship between Buddhist ideals and the natural world can be explored within three contexts:

1. Nature as teacher
2. Nature as a spiritual force
3. Nature as a way of life.

Nature as teacher

Like the Buddha, we too should look around us and be observant, because everything in the world is ready to teach us. With even a little intuitive wisdom we will be able to see clearly through the ways of the world. We will come to understand that everything in the world is a teacher. Trees and vines, for example, can all reveal the true nature of reality. With wisdom there is no need to question anyone, no need to study. We can learn from Nature enough to be enlightened, because everything follows the way of Truth. It does not diverge from Truth. (Ajahn Chah, Forest Sangha Newsletter)

Buddha taught that respect for life and the natural world is essential. By living simply one can be in harmony with other creatures and learn to appreciate the interconnectedness of all that lives. This simplicity of life involves developing openness to our environment and relating to the world with awareness and responsive perception. It enables us to enjoy without possessing, and mutually benefit each other without manipulation.

However, the Buddha was no romantic idealist. He also saw and realized that every living thing is suffering. He saw creatures struggling for survival in a precarious world. He saw death and fear, the strong preying on the weak, and the devastation of thousands of beings as one lonely figure plowed the earth to reap the harvest. He also saw impermanence. As Ajahn Chah has written:

Take trees for example . . . first they come into being, then they grow and mature, constantly changing, until they finally die as every tree must. In the same way, people and animals are born, grow and change during their lifetimes until they eventually die. The multitudinous changes which occur during this transition from birth to death show the Way of Dharma. That is to say, all things are impermanent, having decay and dissolution as their natural condition. (Buddha-Nature)

Nature is not independent and unchanging and neither are we. Change is the very essence of nature. In the words of Stephen Batchelor:

We each believe we are a solid and lasting self rather than a short-term bundle of thoughts, feelings and impulses. (The Sands of the Ganges)

We do not exist independently, separate from everything else—all things in the universe come into existence, "arise" as a result of particular conditions. It is surely a mistake to see fulfillment in terms of external or personal development alone.

Buddha taught us to live simply, to cherish tranquillity, to appreciate the natural cycle of life. In this universe of energies, everything affects everything else. Nature is an ecosystem in which trees affect climate, the soil, and the animals, just as the climate affects the trees, the soil, the animals, and so on. The ocean, the sky, the air are all interrelated and interdependent—water is life and air is life. A result of Buddhist practice is that one does not feel that one's existence is so much more important than anyone else's. The notions of ego clinging, the importance of the individual and emphasis on self is, in the West, a dominant outlook which is moving to the East as "development" and consumerism spread. Instead of looking at things as a seamless undivided whole we tend to categorize and compartmentalize. Instead of seeing nature as our great teacher we waste and do not replenish and forget that Buddha learned his "wisdom from nature."

Once we treat nature as our friend, to cherish it, then we can see the need to change from the attitude of dominating nature to an attitude of working with nature—we are an intrinsic part of all existence rather than seeing ourselves as in control of it.

Nature as a spiritual force

For Shantiveda in eighth-century India, dwelling in nature was obviously preferable to living in a monastery or town:

When shall I come to dwell in forests
Amongst the deer, the birds and the trees,
That say nothing unpleasant
And are delightful to associate with.
(A Guide to the Bodhisattva's Way of Life)

Patrul Rinpoche, one of the greatest Tibetan Buddhist teachers of the nineteenth century, writes:

Base your mind on the Dharma,
Base your Dharma on a humble life,
Base your humble life on the thought of death,
Base your death on a lonely cave.
(The Words of My Perfect Teacher)

The Buddha taught that the balance of nature is achieved by the functions of the forest. Survival of the forest is vital to the survival of natural harmony, balance, morality, and environment.

Buddhist teachers and masters have constantly reminded us of the importance of living in tune with nature, to respect all life, to make time for meditation practice, to live simply and use nature as a spiritual force. Buddha stressed the four boundless qualities: loving-kindness, compassion, sympathetic joy (delight in the well-being of others), and equanimity (impartiality).

Venerable Asabho has spoken of the value of living in retreat in Hammer Woods, Chithurst, England. The forest has its own rhythms and after a few days the metabolism and sleeping patterns adjust and the senses begin to sharpen to this new and unfamiliar setting. Ear and nose play a more important role when not having any comforts of life—gas, electricity, artificial light, and the like. Living in the fast and furious pace of the twentieth century our true nature is often dulled by the massive sensory impact unavoidable in modern urbanized living. Living close to nature is a very healing experience—to have few activities, few distractions. Learning to trust yourself and being more of a friend than a judge one develops a lightness of being, a light confidence. One realizes the truth of the notion of impermanence—the sound of animals, the texture of trees, the subtle changes in the forest and land, the subtle changes in your own mind. A retreat, or simply living in the forest with nature,

> helps people get back to earth, to calm you down—just living with the unhurried rhythms of nature. With nature, everything—birth, growth, degeneration and decay is just as it is, and in that holistic sense everything is all right. Touching lightly is the right touch, the natural touch in which blame, praise, crises, retreats, progress, delays are just as it is and so all right. (Talks given at Chithurst Buddhist Monastery)

Living in this way we can appreciate the fragility of all we love, the fickleness of security. Retreat and solitude complement our religious practice and give the opportunity of deepening, refining, and strengthening the mind. By being mindful about the daily routine one pays attention to the flow of life—to see nature as a positive, joyful, spiritual force.

Nature as a way of life

The Buddha commended frugality as a virtue in its own right. Skillful living avoids waste and we should try to recycle as much as we can. Buddhism advocates a simple, gentle, nonaggressive attitude toward nature—reverence for all forms of nature must be cultivated.

Buddha used examples from nature to teach. In his stories the plant and animal worlds are treated as part of our inheritance, even as part of ourselves. As Krishnamurti said, "We are the world, the world is us." By starting to look at ourselves and the lives we are living we may come to appreciate that the real solution to the environmental crisis begins with us. Craving and greed only bring unhappiness—simplicity, moderation, and the middle way bring liberation and hence equanimity and happiness. Our demands for material possessions can never be satisfied—we will always need to acquire more, there is not enough in the universe to truly satisfy us and give us complete satisfaction and contentment, and no government can fulfil all our desires for security.

Buddhism, however, takes us away from the ethos of the individual and its bondage to materialism and consumerism. When we try to conquer greed and desire we can start to have inner peace and be at peace with those around us. The teaching of the Buddha, the reflections on Dharma, relate to life as it actually is. We are instructed to be mindful—receptive, open, sensitive, and not fixed to any one thing, but able to fix on things according to what is needed in that time and at that place.

By developing the right actions of not killing, stealing, or committing misconduct in sexual desires, perhaps we can begin to live with nature, without breaking it or injuring the rhythm of life. In our livelihoods, by seeking work that does not harm other beings and refraining from trading in weapons, breathing things, meat, alcohol, and poisons, we can feel more at one with nature.

Our minds can be so full, so hyperactive, we never allow ourselves a chance to slow down to be aware of our thoughts, feelings, and emotions, to live fully in the present moment. We need to live as the Buddha taught us to live, in peace and harmony with nature, but this must start with ourselves. If we are going to save this planet, we need to seek a new ecological order, to look at the life we lead and then work together for the benefit of all; unless we work together no solution can be found. By moving away from self-centeredness, sharing wealth more, being more responsible for ourselves, and agreeing to live more simply, we can help decrease much of the suffering in the world. As the Indian philosopher Nagarjuna said, "Things derive their being and nature by mutual dependence and are nothing in themselves."

Breathing in, I know I'm breathing in.
Breathing out, I know
as the in-breath grows deep,
the out-breath grows slow.
Breathing in makes me calm.
Breathing out makes me ease.
With the in-breath, I smile.
With the out-breath, I release.
Breathing in, there is only the present moment
Breathing out is a wonderful moment.
(From a poem by the Venerable Thich Nhat Hanh)

9

Christianity

This statement was compiled and endorsed by the Ecumenical Patriarchate of Constantinople, the World Council of Churches, and the Vatican Franciscan Center of Environmental Studies.

✝ Christianity teaches that all of creation is the loving action of God, who not only willed the creation but also continues to care for all aspects of existence. As Jesus says in the Gospel of Luke (12: 6–7):

> Are not five sparrows sold for two pennies? Yet not one of them is forgotten by God. Indeed the very hairs of your head are all numbered.

Yet sadly, many Christians have been more interested in the last part of what Jesus said:

> Don't be afraid, you are worth more than many sparrows.

There exists within Christianity a tension between God's creative, loving powers and humanity's capacity and tendency to rebel against God. Christianity, drawing upon the biblical imagery of Genesis 1 and 2 and Genesis 9, is unambiguous about the special role of humanity within creation. But this special role has sometimes been interpreted as giving free rein to mastership. As the World Council of Churches said in a document from a meeting in Granvollen, Norway, in 1988:

> The drive to have "mastery" over creation has resulted in the senseless exploitation of natural resources, the alienation of the land from people and the destruction of indigenous cultures. . . . Creation came into being by the will and love of the Triune God, and as such it possesses an inner cohesion and goodness. Though human eyes may not always discern it,

every creature and the whole creation in chorus bear witness to the glorious unity and harmony with which creation is endowed. And when our human eyes are opened and our tongues unloosed, we too learn to praise and participate in the life, love, power and freedom that is God's continuing gift and grace.

In differing ways, the main churches have sought to either revise or reexamine their theology and as a result their practice in the light of the environmental crisis. For example, Pope Paul VI in his Apostolic Letter, Octogesima Adveniens, also comments in a similar manner:

> By an ill-considered exploitation of nature he [humanity] risks destroying it and becoming in his turn the victim of this degradation . . . flight from the land, industrial growth, continual demographic expansion and the attraction of urban centers bring about concentrations of population difficult to imagine.

In his 1990 New Year's message, His Holiness the Pope also stated: "Christians, in particular, realize that their responsibility within creation and their duty toward nature and the Creator are an essential part of their faith."

In Orthodoxy this is brought out even more strongly, especially in the document produced by the Ecumenical Patriarchate, *Orthodoxy and the Ecological Crisis*, in 1990. The Orthodox Church teaches that humanity, both individually and collectively, ought to perceive the natural order as a sign and sacrament of God. This is obviously not what happens today. Rather, humanity perceives the natural order as an object of exploitation. There is no one who is not guilty of disrespecting nature, for to respect nature is to recognize that all creatures and objects have a unique place in God's creation. When we become sensitive to God's world around us, we grow more conscious also of God's world within us. Beginning to see nature as a work of God, we begin to see our own place as human beings within nature. The true appreciation of any object is to discover the extraordinary in the ordinary.

The Orthodox Church teaches that it is the destiny of humanity to restore the proper relationship between God and the world as it was in Eden. Through repentance, two landscapes—the one human, the other natural—can become the objects of a caring and creative effort. But repentance must be accompanied by soundly focused initiatives that manifest the ethos of Orthodox Christian faith.

The World Council of Churches, predominantly Protestant, but also with full Orthodox participation, issued the following when they called their member churches together in 1990 to consider the issues of justice, peace, and the integrity of creation:

Affirmation VII

We affirm the creation as beloved of God.

We affirm that the world, as God's handiwork, has its own inherent integrity; that land, waters, air, forests, mountains and all creatures, including humanity, are "good" in God's sight. The integrity of creation has a social aspect which we recognize as peace with justice, and an ecological aspect which we recognize in the self-renewing, sustainable character of natural ecosystems.

We will resist the claim that anything in creation is merely a resource for human exploitation. We will resist species extinction for human benefit; consumerism and harmful mass production; pollution of land, air and waters; all human activities which are now leading to probable rapid climate change; and the policies and plans which contribute to the disintegration of creation.

Therefore we commit ourselves to be members of both the living community of creation in which we are but one species, and members of the covenant community of Christ; to be full co-workers with God, with moral responsibility to respect the rights of future generations; and to conserve and work for the integrity of creation both for its inherent value to God and in order that justice may be achieved and sustained.

Implicit in these affirmations is the belief that it has been human selfishness, greed, foolishness, or even perversity that has wrought destruction and death upon so much of the planet. This is also central to Christian understanding. As far as we can tell, human beings are the only species capable of rebelling against what God has revealed as the way in which we should live. This rebellion takes many forms, but one of these is the abuse of the rest of creation. Christians are called to recognize their need to be liberated from those forces within themselves and within society that militate against a loving and just relationship one with another and between humans and the rest of creation. The need to repent for what has been done and to hope that change can really transform the situation are two sides of the same coin. The one without the other becomes defeatist or romantic—neither of which is ultimately of much use to the rest of the world.

The Orthodox Churches pursue this in their own line of theology and reflection concerning creation, and expressed their commitment in the document *Orthodoxy and the Ecological Crisis:*

We must attempt to return to a proper relationship with the Creator AND the creation. This may well mean that just as a shepherd will in times of greatest hazard, lay down his life for his flock, so human beings may need to forego part of their wants and needs in order that the survival of the natural world can be assured. This is a new situation—a new challenge. It calls for humanity to bear some of the pain of creation as well as to enjoy and celebrate it. It calls first and foremost for repentance—but of an order not previously understood by many. (10–11)

The hope comes from a model of our relationship with nature that turns the power we so often use for destruction into a sacrificial or servant power, here using the image of the priest at the Eucharist:

> Just as the priest at the Eucharist offers the fullness of creation and receives it back as the blessing of Grace in the form of the consecrated bread and wine, to share with others, so we must be the channel through which God's grace and deliverance is shared with all creation. The human being is simply yet gloriously means for the expression of creation in its fullness and the coming of God's deliverance for all creation. (8)

For Christians, the very act of creation and the love of God in Christ for all creation stands as a constant reminder that, while we humans are special, we are also just a part of God's story of creation. To quote again from the World Council of Churches, from the report of the 1991 General Assembly on the theme "Come Holy Spirit—Renew the Whole Creation":

> The divine presence of the Spirit in creation binds us human beings together with all created life. We are accountable before God in and to the community of life, an accountability which has been imagined in various ways: as servants, stewards and trustees, as tillers and keepers, as priests of creation, as nurturers, as co-creators. This requires attitudes of compassion and humility, respect and reverence.

For some Christians, the way forward lies in a rediscovery of distinctive teachings, lifestyles, and insights contained within their tradition. For others, it requires a radical rethinking of what it means to be Christian. For yet others, there is still a struggle to reconcile centuries of human-centered Christian teaching with the truths that the environmentalists are telling us about the state of the world we are responsible for creating. For all of them, the core remains the belief in the Creator God who so loved the world that he sent his only begotten Son, that whoever believes in him should have eternal life (John 3:16). In the past, we can now see, this promise of life eternal has often been interpreted by the churches as meaning only human life. The challenge to all Christians is to discover anew the truth that God's love and liberation is for all creation, not just humanity; to realize that we should have been stewards, priests, co-creators with God for the rest of creation but have actually often been the ones responsible for its destruction; and to seek new ways of living and being Christians that will restore that balance and give the hope of life to so much of the endangered planet.

10

Daoism

The China Daoist Association, based at White Cloud Temple in Beijing, is the leading body representing all Daoists in mainland China. This piece is an authoritative statement by the Association.

Daoism emerged on the basis of what are known as the One Hundred Schools of Thought during the period 770–221 B.C. Starting with the formal setting up of Daoist organizations in the East Han period (A.D. 25–220), the faith has a history of nearly 2,000 years. Daoism has been one of the main components of Chinese traditional culture, and it has exerted great influence on the Chinese people's way of thinking, working, and acting. It is no exaggeration to say that in every Chinese person's consciousness and subconscious, the factors of Daoism exist to a greater or lesser degree.

Because of its deep cultural roots and its great social impact, Daoism is now one of the five recognized religions in China (the others are Buddhism, Catholicism, Islam, and Protestantism). Even more, the influence of Daoism has already transcended the Chinese-speaking world and has attracted international attention.

According to our statistics, more than 1,000 Daoist temples have now opened to the public (this number does not include those in Taiwan, Hong Kong, and Macao), and about 10,000 Daoists live in such communities. There are about 100 Daoist associations all over China, affiliated with the China Daoist Association. Several colleges have also been established to train Daoists, and many books and periodicals on the study and teaching of Daoism have been published. All Daoists work hard in order that Daoism should develop and flourish. They take an active part in mobilizing the masses, carrying forward the best in Daoist tradition, and working for the benefit of human society.

Like every major world religion, Daoism has its own outlook on the universe, human life, ideals of virtue, and ultimate purpose. Due to its distinctive cultural and historical background, it has its own striking characteristics. It can be briefly summarized in the following two precepts:

1. Give respect to the Dao above everything else.

Dao simply means "the way." Daoism considers that Dao is the origin of everything, and Dao is the ultimate aim of all Daoists. This is the most fundamental tenet of Daoism. Dao is the way of Heaven, Earth, and Humanity. The Dao took form in the being of the Grandmother Goddess. She came to Earth to enlighten humanity. She taught the people to let everything grow according to its own course without any interference. This is called the way of no action, no selfishness (wu-wei), and this principle is an important rule for Daoists. It teaches them to be very plain and modest, and not to struggle with others for personal gain in their material life. This kind of virtue is the ideal spiritual kingdom for which the followers of Daoism long.

2. Give great value to life.

Daoism pursues immortality. It regards life as the most valuable thing. Master Zhang Daoling (c. second century A.D.) said that life is another expression of Dao, and the study of Dao includes the study of how to extend one's life. With this principle in mind, many Daoists have undertaken considerable exploration in this regard. They believe that life is not controlled by Heaven, but by human beings themselves. People can prolong life through meditation and exercise. The exercises include both the moral and the physical sides. People should train their will, discard selfishness and the pursuit of fame, do good deeds, and seek to become a model of virtue (de).

Daoism considers that the enhancement of virtue is the precondition and the first aim of practicing the Dao. The achievement of immortality is a reward from the gods for practicing worthy acts. With a high moral sense and with systematic exercise in accordance with the Daoist method and philosophy of life, people can keep sufficient life essence and energy in their bodies all their lives. The Daoist exercise of achieving immortality has proved very effective in practice. It can keep people younger and in good health. But there is one point that cannot be neglected: a peaceful and harmonious natural environment is a very important external condition.

Daoist ideas about nature

With the deepening world environmental crisis, more and more people have come to realize that the problem of the environment not only is brought about by modern industry and technology, but also has a deep connection with people's world outlook, with their sense of value, and with the way they structure knowledge. Some people's ways of thinking have, in certain ways, unbalanced the harmonious relationship between human beings and nature, and overstressed the power and influence of the human will. People think that nature can be rapaciously exploited.

This philosophy is the ideological root of the current serious environmental and ecological crisis. On the one hand, it brings about high productivity; on the other hand, it brings about an exaggerated sense of one's own importance. Confronted with the destruction of the Earth, we have to conduct a thorough self-examination on this way of thinking.

We believe that Daoism has teachings that can be used to counteract the shortcomings of currently prevailing values. Daoism looks upon humanity as the most intelligent and creative entity in the universe (which is seen as encompassing humanity, Heaven, and Earth within the Dao).

There are four main principles that should guide the relationship between humanity and nature:

1. In the Dao De Jing, the basic classic of Daoism, there is this verse: "Humanity follows the Earth, the Earth follows Heaven, Heaven follows the Dao, and the Dao follows what is natural." This means that the whole of humanity should attach great importance to the Earth and should obey its rule of movement. The Earth has to respect the changes of Heaven, and Heaven must abide by the Dao. And the Dao follows the natural course of development of everything. So we can see that what human beings can do with nature is to help everything grow according to its own way. We should cultivate in people's minds the way of no action in relation to nature, and let nature be itself.

2. In Daoism, everything is composed of two opposite forces known as Yin and Yang. Yin represents the female, the cold, the soft, and so forth; Yang represents the male, the hot, the hard, and so on. The two forces are in constant struggle within everything. When they reach harmony, the energy of life is created. From this we can see how important harmony is to nature. Someone who understands this point will see and act intelligently. Otherwise, people will probably violate the law of nature and destroy the harmony of nature.

   There are generally two kinds of attitude toward the treatment of nature, as is said in another classic of Daoism, Bao Pu Zi (written in the fourth century A.D.). One attitude is to make full use of nature, the other is to observe and follow nature's way. Those who have only a superficial understanding of the relationship between humanity and nature will recklessly exploit nature. Those who have a deep understanding of the relationship will treat nature well and learn from it. For example, some Daoists have studied the way of the crane and the turtle, and have imitated their methods of exercise to build up their own constitutions. It is obvious that in the long run, the excessive use of nature will bring about disaster, even the extinction of humanity.

3. People should take into full consideration the limits of nature's sustaining power, so that when they pursue their own development, they have a correct standard of success. If anything runs counter to the harmony and balance of nature, even if it is of great immediate interest and profit, people should restrain themselves from doing it, so as to prevent nature's punishment. Furthermore, insatiable human desire will lead to the overexploitation of natural resources. So people should remember that to be too successful is to be on the path to defeat.

4. Daoism has a unique sense of value in that it judges affluence by the number of different species. If all things in the universe grow well, then a society is a community of affluence. If not, this kingdom is on the decline. This view encourages both government and people to take good care of nature. This thought is a very special contribution by Daoism to the conservation of nature.

To sum up, many Daoist ideas still have positive significance for the present world. We sincerely hope that the thoughts of all religions that are conducive to the human being will be promoted, and will be used to help humanity build harmonious relationships between people and nature. In this way eternal peace and development can be maintained in the world.

11
Hinduism

This statement is based on papers and comments by Dr. Sheshagiri Rao, chief editor of The Encyclopaedia of Hinduism; *Swami Chidananda Sarasvati, founder of the India Heritage Research Foundation, spiritual head of Parmarth Niketan Ashram; Shrivatsa Goswami, Vaishnava Acharya of Shri Radharaman Temple, Vrindavan chairman of the Vrindavan Conservation Project; and Swami Vibudhesha Teertha, Acharya of Madhvacarya Vaishnavas, Udupi, central advisory committee member of the Visva Hindu Parishad.*

ॐ This statement consists of three sections reflecting the major strands within Vedic—known in the West as Hindu—thought.

Sustaining the balance—Swami Vibudhesha Teertha

These days it looks as if human beings have forgotten that a particular natural condition on Earth enabled life to come into existence and evolve to the human level. Humanity is disturbing this natural condition on which our existence, along with the existence of all other forms of life, depends. This is like the action of a woodcutter cutting a tree at the trunk, on the branch on which he is sitting. According to Hindu religion, "dharanath dharma ucyate"—that which sustains all species of life and helps to maintain harmonious relationship among them is dharma. That which disturbs such ecology is adharma.

Hindu religion wants its followers to live a simple life. It does not allow people to go on increasing their material wants. People are meant to learn to enjoy spiritual happiness, so that to derive a sense of satisfaction and fulfilment, they need not run after material pleasures and disturb nature's checks and balances. They have to milk a cow and enjoy, not cut at the udder of the cow with greed to enjoy what is not available in the natural course. Do not use anything belonging to nature, such as oil, coal, or forest, at a greater rate than you can replenish it. For example, do not destroy birds, fish, earthworms, and even bacteria which play vital ecological roles; once they are annihilated you cannot recreate them. Thus only can you avoid becoming bankrupt, and the life cycle can continue for a long, long time.

"Conserve ecology or perish" is the message of the Bhagavad Gita, a dialogue between Sri Krishna and Arjuna that is a clear and precise Life Science. It is narrated in the third chapter of this great work that a life without contribution toward the preservation of ecology is a life of sin and a life without specific purpose or use. The ecological cycle is explained in verses 3:14–16:

> Living bodies subsist on food grains, which are produced from rains. Rains are produced from performance of yajna [sacrifice], and yajna is born of prescribed duties. Regulated activities are prescribed in the Vedas, and the Vedas are directly manifested from the Supreme Personality of Godhead. Consequently the all-pervading Transcendence is eternally situated in acts of sacrifice. My dear Arjuna, one who does not follow in human life the cycle of sacrifice thus established by the Vedas certainly lives a life full of sin. Living only for the satisfaction of the senses, such a person lives in vain.

Life is sustained by different kinds of food; rainfall produces food; timely movement of clouds brings rains; to get the clouds moving on time yajna, religious sacrifice, helps; yajna is performed through rituals; those actions that produce rituals belong only to God; God is revealed by the Vedas; the Vedas are preserved by the human mind; and the human mind is nourished by food. This is the cycle that helps the existence of all forms of life on this globe. One who does not contribute to the maintenance of this cycle is considered as a destroyer of all life here. When the Lord desired to create life, He created the Sun, Moon, and Earth, and through them a congenial atmosphere for life to come into being. Therefore the Sun, Moon, Earth, Stars, and all objects in the universe jointly, not individually, create the atmosphere for the creation, sustenance, or destruction of everything in the universe. The Earth is the only daughter of the Sun to produce children. The Moon is essential for the creation of the right atmosphere for those children to exist and evolve. This we say because of the influence of the Moon on high and low tides in our rivers and oceans. This is narrated also in the Bhagavad Gita:

> I become the moon and thereby supply the juice of life to all vegetables.

We cannot refute this influence of the Moon on life. It is proved by the movement of all liquid on this globe depending on the movement of the Moon. Therefore ecology in totality must be preserved: just a part of it would not suffice.

Hinduism is a religion that is very near to nature. It asks its followers to see God in every object in the Universe. Worship of God in air, water, fire, Sun, Moon, Stars, and Earth is specially recommended. Earth is worshipped as the spouse of God, hence very dear and near to God. All lives on Earth are considered as children of God and Earth.

Sri Krishna in the Bhagavad Gita says,

> I am pervading the Universe. All objects in the Universe rest on me as pearls on the thread of a garland.

The Upanishads narrate that after creating the Universe, the Creator entered into each and every object to help them maintain their interrelationship. The Upanishad says "tat sristva ta devanu pravisat": after creating the universe He entered into every object created. Therefore to contribute toward the maintenance of this interrelationship becomes worship of God. Hindus believe that there is soul in all plants and animals. One has to do penance even for killing plants and animals for food. This daily penance is called visva deva. Visva deva is nothing but an offering of prepared food to the Creator, asking His pardon.

The Hindu religion gives great importance to protecting cattle. At every Hindu house there is a cow and it is worshipped. The cow is a great friend of humans. It nourishes us through its milk and provides manure to grow our food. This it does without any extra demand—it lives on the fodder got while growing our food. Advanced countries have started to realize the harmful effects of consuming food grown with chemical manure. When we use chemical manure, the top soil loses its fertility. This generation has no right to use up all the fertility of the soil and leave behind an unproductive land for future generations.

There is no life that is inferior. All lives enjoy the same importance in the Universe and all play their fixed roles. They are to function together and no link in the chain is to be lost. If some link is lost, the whole ecological balance would be disturbed. All kinds of life—insects, birds, and animals—contribute toward the maintenance of ecological balance, but what is man's contribution toward this? We are an intelligent animal; therefore our contribution should be the biggest. But we find the absence of our contribution. On the other hand, we are nullifying the benefits of the contributions made by other species of life. We are disturbing the balance because of our greed for material enjoyment and our craze for power. We do not allow earthworms and bacteria to maintain the fertility of the soil by using chemical manures and insecticides which kill them. We destroy plants and forests indiscriminately and come in the way of plants providing oxygen essential for the very existence of life. By destroying plants and forests we become an agent for increasing the deadly carbon dioxide in the atmosphere. We pollute the air by burning oil for all sorts of machines. We produce unhealthy sounds through our various machineries and instruments which cause sound pollution. By building towns and cities on the banks of rivers, we pollute all water in rivers. The Hindu religion holds all rivers as holy; polluting them is a big sin. Hinduism encourages the planting of trees like Tulasi, Neem, Peepal, and the like which are rich in medicinal properties.

Rishis gave the navel to Brahma, the creator, and to the sustainer Vishnu they gave the heart as His abode. The destroyer, Shiva, is given control of the brain. By doing this they wanted us to know that the language of the heart only can sustain us—when we start speaking through the language of the mind our destruction becomes inevitable. Therefore, a thinking animal has to be very careful while it uses its mental abilities: these are to be applied only with spiritual background. Mind is to act as our friend and not as our enemy. It is to function under our control; we should not succumb to its control. "Mana eva manusyanam karanam bandha moksayoh": for man, mind is the cause of bondage and mind is the cause of liberation (Amrita Bindhu Upanishad 2).

There should be a purpose for the creation of humanity. What it might be! We could be the sustainer of interrelationship among numerous life species on Earth. We could be the ones who see God, and all objects, as the controller and sustainer of ecological balance. All other animals play their roles without knowing what they are doing, but we do everything with full consciousness. God created our minds to see His own reflection as in a mirror. Our minds can meditate on God and know him more and more. When we develop consciousness of the presence of God and His continuous showering of blessings on the universe, we develop deep love for Him. To enjoy this nectar of love, God created us. Only we have time-space conception. Therefore, we only can see God, pervading time and space, conserving the ecological balance which is the greatest boon bestowed on the universe by God. Though we cannot contribute toward the conservation in the same way as other animals do, we can help all lives and other objects in the universe to play their roles effectively by persuading God through prayers of love to grant them the required energy and directions. "Yavat bhumandalam datte samrigavana karnanam, tavat tisthati medhinyam santatih putra pautriki": so long as the Earth preserves her forests and wildlife, our progeny will continue to exist. This is the Hindu approach toward the conservation of ecology.

Sacrifice and protection—Dr. Sheshagiri Rao

Sacrifice

The Creator, in the beginning, created humans together with sacrifice, and said, "By this you shall multiply. Let this be your cow of plenty and give you the milk of your desires. With sacrifice you will nourish the gods, and the gods will nourish you. Thus you will obtain the Highest Good (Bhagavad Gita 3:10–11).

Sacrifice does not just mean ritual worship—it means an act that protects life. Personal health depends on eyes, ears, and other sense organs working together in harmony; human prosperity and happiness depend on a well-ordered society and nature; the universe is sustained by the cosmic powers such as the sun and moon working together in unison. Sacrifice reinvigorates the powers that sustain the world by securing cosmic stability and social order. It activates the positive forces of the universe and protects the Earth from degeneration.

Nonviolence

God's creation is sacred. Humanity does not have the right to destroy what it cannot create. Humans have to realize the interconnectedness of living entities and emphasize the idea of moral responsibility to oneself, one's society, and the world as a whole. In our cosmic journey, we are involved in countless cycles of births and deaths. Life progresses into higher forms or regresses into lower forms of life based upon our good or bad karma. Kinship exists between all forms of life. Reincarnation warns us against treating lower forms of life with cruelty.

Cow protection

Human beings have evolved from lower forms of life. They are, therefore, related to the whole creation. The principle of cow protection symbolizes human responsibility to the subhuman world. It also indicates reverence for all forms of life. The cow serves humans throughout its life, and even after death. The milk of the cow runs in our blood. Its contributions to the welfare of the family and the community are countless. Hindus pray daily for the welfare of cows. When the cows are cared for, the world at all levels will find happiness and peace.

Earth as mother

Hindus revere the Earth as mother. She feeds, shelters, and clothes us. Without her we cannot survive. If we as children do not take care of her, we diminish her ability to take care of us. Unfortunately the Earth herself is now being undermined by our scientific and industrial achievements.

Breaking the family—Shrivatsa Goswami

Let there be peace in the heavens, the Earth, the atmosphere, the water, the herbs, the vegetation, among the divine beings and in Brahman, the absolute reality. Let everything be at peace and in peace. Only then will we find peace.

According to Hindu philosophy, the goal of human life is the realization of the state of peace. Dharma, loosely translated as religion, is the source by which peace can be fully realized. This peace is not the stillness of death; it is a dynamic harmony among all the diverse facets of life. Humanity, as part of the natural world, can contribute through dharma to this natural harmony.

The natural harmony that should exist in the play of energies between humanity and the natural world is now disrupted by the weakest player in the game—humanity. Although it is the totality of this game that provides our nourishment, through ignorance of our own natural limits we destroy this source of nourishment.

This awareness of ecological play or playful ecology is inseparable from awareness of the need for friendship and play as the real basis for human relationship. The family within which these relationships are nourished is not limited to its human members. Just as the human child has to be nourished by Mother Nature, and the human spirit has to be embraced and loved by beautiful nature, so the human being who has grown old or sick has to be supported by caring nature. If humans distress the mother, rape the beauty, and beat the caring nurse, what happens? The relationship collapses, and the family is broken.

The Sanskrit for family is parivara, and environment is paryavarana. If we think of the environment as our home and all of its members as our family, it is clear that the key to conserving nature is devotion, love—giving and serving. Nature, prakriti, as the feminine can give and serve. But the role of humanity, purusha, is then to protect. Nowadays purusha, humanity, is interested not in protecting but in exploiting, so prakriti, nature, has to defend herself. This is why we see nature in her furious manifestation—in drought, floods, or hurricanes. If we rape the mother's womb, she has convulsions, and we blame her for devastating earthquakes. If we denude her of her lush hair and beautiful skin, she punishes us by withholding food and water.

As it is through ignorance that we destroy our relationships in the family and within the environment, that ignorance becomes the root cause of our suffering. The best way to get rid of this ignorance is to unlearn what is wrong. This unlearning is shaped not only in the school but in the family and community, and it has to begin with the very young.

Traditional Hindu education covers all facets of life—economic, political, cultural, and above all religious. Whether we speak of Krishna, of Chaitanya, or of Gandhi, we see that they drew no clear division between the economic or political and the religious or cultural facets of life. The body and mind are in the service of the heart. In the same way politics and economics are rooted in and guided by religion and culture, and ultimately by spiritual experience.

12
Islam

Muhammad Hyder Ihsan Mahasneh is a biologist and Islamic scholar and was the first African head of the Kenya National Parks Service. He was appointed by the Muslim World League to compile this paper.

Humanity's most primordial concepts of religion relate to the environment. Human history on planet Earth is, on a geological scale, very short indeed. Planet Earth itself is a mere 3,800 million years old; human beings only appeared 1 million or maybe 2 million years ago. Most of the physical patterns of planet Earth were probably in place, broadly speaking, by the time humans evolved. Apart from what they first saw, they also probably witnessed some spectacular changes themselves. They must, at the very least, have gone through one Ice Age and seen some graphic volcanic eruptions—assuming they were able to avoid the consequences. The environment, therefore, very probably induced the first thoughts of a Super-Being—a God, if you like—whose manifestations lay in human beings' immediate surroundings.

The environment also provided another dimension in humanity's relationship with nature. To survive in a given environment, humans have to adjust what they take from that environment to what can give them sustainable yields on (at the very least) an annual basis. In effect this meant that early humans had to learn to conserve at an early age. Being largely dependent on what was available rather than on what they could cultivate, they entered into a partnership with the environment. To take more than the regenerative capacity of the environment could replace could lead to serious subsequent exhaustion—quite rightly seen as harsh retribution from an angry God. The converse situation of exploitation with moderation led to sustained yields which were (again, quite rightly) taken as having pleased God.

This relationship between conservation and religion is thus not only a natural one but also probably as old as the proverbial hills. But when we quickly open most of the pages of human history on planet Earth and come to the past 300 years or so, we find the advent of the Industrial Revolution. The Industrial Revolution made possible the production of large quantities of goods in a very short time. That meant that raw materials in ever-increasing quantities had to be found to feed the hungry mills ready to convert them into finished or semi-finished goods. The consequences of the Industrial Revolution were many—economic, social, and environmental. The material achievements of the human race in the past 100 or so years have overshadowed the contributions made by all past civilizations. The Industrial Revolution that took place in Europe in the eighteenth and nineteenth centuries exacted a high social and environmental cost. Now these costs are even higher and more universal, being manifestly so in the great urban centers of the world. The paradox of "progress" today is the easily perceived correlation between complex consumer societies and the degeneration of the human being. Or as John Seymour puts it:

> We see men now wherever we look, so blinded by arrogance and the worship of man as God that they are doing things no one but the insane would do . . . men maddened by the belief that they are both omniscient and omnipotent, that they are indeed, God.

The Industrial Revolution also proclaimed a new revival of another God: Mammon. Mammon regrettably has no respect for environmental integrity—nor do his followers. The last 250 years have seen a growing decimation of ever more pristine areas of nature to feed the insatiable industrial cuckoo and its resultant consumerism. Forests—particularly tropical forests—have been systematically hewn down, the seas ransacked, the lands made totally dependent on a host of inorganic fertilizers and pesticides for food production. Wastes galore have filled the seas, the rivers, and the lakes, not to mention the landfills.

We must also take note that the "unmatched material progress" of this century that we are often fond of talking about has only been possible for the few: that is, the population of the Northern Hemisphere and a small minority among the peoples of the South. This is usually translated as less than 25 percent of the world's population consuming over 75 percent of the world's resources. This rate of consumption by a minority of the human species has caused unparalleled climatic change, ecosystem disintegration, and species extinction. As a report by the World Wide Fund for Nature observes:

> Loss of biodiversity worldwide, and the combination of global warming with other human pressures will present the greatest challenge in conservation for decades to come.

This would lead us to conclude that there is a profound and inherent contradiction in the efforts made by the "North" to keep ahead of the rest as consumers, and the push by the remaining 75 percent of the world's population to catch up. Given this scenario, if Eastern Europe or Russia or India or China alone managed to raise its standard of living by just a few percentage points, then the consequences of putting this extra load on the earth's ecosystem, which is already under severe strain, would be catastrophic.

This is the background against which the followers of the relatively ancient, environmentally conscious (indeed environmentally concerned) God have gathered to reexamine and to restate their own commitment to environmental integrity from their own individual religion's standpoint. We for our part will look at the underpinnings of conservation in Islam.

Islam and conservation

There are several Islamic principles that, when taken individually, seem to have little bearing on conservation. Together, however, they add up to a clear concept of the Islamic view on conservation. We shall now annotate these principles briefly.

Tawheed

The first Islamic principle that relates to conservation is that of the Oneness of Allah, or Tawheed. This principle is absolutely fundamental to Islam. Every Muslim must believe in this Oneness of Allah. It is said by some Ulamaa that some two-thirds of Prophet Muhammad's (SAW) early preaching—and indeed of the Qur'an itself—were and are dedicated purely to endorsing this very Oneness of Allah. One indivisible God means to a Muslim that there is no separate deity for each of the many attributes that to Muslims belong to the One Universal God who is also God of the Universe.

Tawheed is the monotheistic principle of Islam, and it begins by declaring that "there is no God but God" (the second half of this declaration asserts that "Muhammad is His Messenger"). We are for the present concerned with the first part, which affirms that there is nothing other than the Absolute, the Eternal, All Powerful Creator. This is the bedrock statement of the Oneness of the Creator from which stems everything else.

It is the primordial testimony of the unity of all creation and the interlocking grid of the natural order of which humanity is intrinsically a part.[1]

---

1. Fazlun Khalid, "Islam, Ecology and the World Order" (paper presented at a conference on Islam and the Environment, United Kingdom, 1993).

God says in the Qur'an:[2]

112.001. Say: He is Allah the One and Only;
112.002. Allah the Eternal Absolute;
112.003. He begetteth not nor is He begotten;
112.004. And there is none like unto Him.

God is Real, not an abstract idea or concept; He is One, the Everlasting Refuge for all creation.

Man's relation to God

The emphasis on Tawheed is significant in itself, but it is even more relevant to the present discussion by virtue of defining a Muslim's relationship to Allah. The Omniscience and Omnipotence of Allah means, by definition, that a Muslim's relationship to Allah is total. To Him—and to Him only—should humans refer for all their needs: physical, mental, and spiritual. Indeed, Allah would not have it any other way. As He says in the Qur'an:

004.048. Allah forgiveth not that partners should be set up with him; but He forgiveth anything else to whom He pleaseth; to set up partners with Allah is to devise a sin most heinous indeed.

But Allah is not only the One Indivisible God. He is also the Universal God as well as the Lord of the Universe:

001.002. Praise be to Allah, Lord of the Worlds.

And again:

006.071. Say: "Allah's guidance is the [only] guidance and we have been directed to submit ourselves to the Lord of the worlds."
006.072. To establish regular prayers and to fear Allah; for it is to Him that we shall be gathered together.
006.073. It is He Who created the heavens and the earth in true [proportions]: the day He saith "Be" Behold! it is. His Word is the truth. His will be the dominion the day the trumpet will be blown. He knoweth the Unseen as well as that which is open. For He is the Wise well acquainted [with all things].

---

2. The numbers at the beginning of each Qur'anic quotation refer to the chapter and verse(s) of the Qur'an. The translation used is by Abdalla Yusuf Ali.

To Allah belongs the earth and the heavens

Yet another principle that underpins Islamic commitment to the conservation of nature and natural resources is the principle of divine ownership of all that exists on earth and in the heavens—animate and inanimate. There are countless verses in the Holy Qur'an that state this. A few are given below.

In the celebrated Ayatul Kursiyy:

002.255. Allah! there is no Allah but He the living the Self subsisting Eternal. No slumber can seize him nor sleep. His are all things in the heavens and on earth. Who is there can intercede in His presence except as He permitteth? He knoweth what [appeareth to his creatures as] before or after or behind them. Nor shall they compass aught of his knowledge except as He willeth. His throne doth extend over the heavens and the earth and He feeleth no fatigue in guarding and preserving them. For He is the Most High the Supreme [in glory].

And again:

004.171. To Him belong all things in the heavens and on earth. And enough is Allah as a Disposer of affairs.
006.013. To Him belongeth all that dwelleth [or lurketh] in the night and the day. For He is the One Who heareth and knoweth all things.
020.006. To Him belongs what is in the heavens and on earth and all between them and all beneath the soil.
021.019. To Him belong all [creatures] in the heavens and on earth: even those who are in His [very] Presence are not too proud to serve Him nor are they [ever] weary [of His service].

But we are reminded that all things animate and inanimate, in their own ways, submit themselves to the Glory of Allah. There are many verses in the Qur'an about this:

030.026. To Him belongs every being that is in the heavens and on earth: all are devoutly obedient to Him.

And again:

062.001. Whatever is in the heavens and on earth doth declare the Praises and Glory of Allah the Sovereign the Holy One the Exalted in Might the Wise.

Thus Allah, the One Indivisible God, the Universal God, and the Lord of the Universe is the Owner also of all that is in the universe, including humanity. After all, we are reminded to say constantly:

002.155. Be sure We shall test you with something of fear and hunger some loss in goods or lives or the fruits [of your toil] but give glad tidings to those who patiently persevere.

002.156. Who say when afflicted with calamity: "To Allah we belong and to Him is our return."

The above set of principles—all taken from Islam's ultimate authority, the Holy Qu'ran—define the perspectives of the relationship of humanity to God and of God to the environment in its totality. A second set of principles that the Holy Qur'an enunciates prescribe man's relationship to the environment after, of course, humanity has accepted the preceding principles.

Humanity and the Khalifa

The most important of this second set of principles is that which defines humans' role and their responsibilities in the natural order that Allah provided. The appointment of each of us as a Khalifa, or guardian, is the sacred duty God has given to the human race. The appointment of humanity to this elevated position gives rise to the one occasion when the Angels actually questioned Allah's decision as seen in the following verses:

002.030. Behold thy Lord said to the angels: "I will create a vice regent on earth." They said "Wilt thou place therein one who will make mischief therein and shed blood? Whilst we do celebrate Thy praises and glorify Thy holy [name]?" He said: "I know what ye know not."

002.031. And He taught Adam the nature of all things; then He placed them before the angels and said: "Tell Me the nature of these if ye are right."

002.032. They said: "Glory to Thee of knowledge we have none save that Thou hast taught us: in truth it is Thou who art perfect in knowledge and wisdom."

002.033. He said: "O Adam I tell them their natures." When he had told them Allah said: "Did I not tell you that I know the secrets of heaven and earth and I know what ye reveal and what ye conceal?"

002.034. And behold We said to the angels: "Bow down to Adam" and they bowed down. Not so Iblis: he refused and was haughty: He was of those who reject Faith.

Clearly Allah preferred the unprogrammed free will of human beings to the pre-programmed goodness of Angels!

And again:

006.165. It is He who hath made you [His] agents inheritors of the earth: He hath raised you in ranks some above others: that he may try you in the gifts He hath given you: for thy Lord is quick in punishment: yet He is indeed Oft-Forgiving Most Merciful.

The exercise of the vice regency is defined in the Qur'an by another set of principles in which our privileges as well as our responsibilities are clearly defined. We shall deal with these briefly in the following paragraphs.

Mizaan

One of the most important attributes conferred on us is the faculty of reasoning. This, above all, might well be the deciding fact in our appointment as God's vice regents on earth. The relevant verses reminding us of this faculty are below:

055.001. [Allah] Most Gracious!
055.002. It is He Who has taught the Qur'an.
055.003. He has created man:
055.004. He has taught him speech [and Intelligence]
055.005. The sun and the moon follow courses [exactly] computed;
055.006. And the herbs and the trees—both [alike] bow in adoration.
055.007. And the firmament has He raised high and He has set up the balance [of Justice]
055.008. In order that ye may not transgress [due] balance.
055.009. So establish weight with justice and fall not short in the balance.
055.010. It is He Who has spread out the earth for [His] creatures:
055.011. Therein is fruit and date-palms producing spathes [enclosing dates]:
055.012. Also corn with [its] leaves and stalk for fodder and sweet-smelling plants.
055.013. Then which of the favors of your Lord will ye deny?

We were not created to function exclusively on instinct. The "explanation" was taught to us because we have the capacity to reason and understand. There is order and purpose in the whole pattern of creation. The Sun and Moon following stable orbits make life possible. The whole universe is in submission to the Creator—the stars that enable us to steer courses and the trees that give us sustenance, shelter, and other uses. The world functions only because creation follows a preordained pattern. We, then, have a responsibility by virtue of being able to reason, to behave justly, "to transgress not in the balance." We owe this to ourselves as much as for the rest of creation.

Justice

The capacity to reason and to balance intellectual judgment would in itself be insufficient without the additional moral commitment to Justice. And this is what the Qur'an prescribes for Muslims:

004.135. O ye who believe! stand out firmly for justice as witnesses to Allah even as against yourselves or your parents or your kin and whether it be [against] rich or poor: for Allah can best protect both. Follow not the lusts [of your hearts] lest ye swerve and if ye distort [justice] or decline to do justice verily Allah is well acquainted with all that ye do.

And again:

004.085. Whoever recommends and helps a good cause becomes a partner therein: and whoever recommends and helps an evil cause shares in its burden: and Allah hath power over all things.
004.058. Allah doth command you to render back your trusts to those to whom they are due; and when ye judge between man and man that ye judge with justice: verily how excellent is the teaching which He giveth you! for Allah is He who heareth and seeth all things.

And again:

005.009. O ye who believe! stand out firmly for Allah as witnesses to fair dealing and let not the hatred of others to you make you swerve to wrong and depart from justice. Be just: that is next to Piety: and fear Allah for Allah is well-acquainted with all that ye do.
005.045. [They are fond of] listening to falsehood of devouring anything forbidden. If they do come to thee either judge between them or decline to interfere. If thou decline they cannot hurt thee in the least. If thou judge judge in equity between them; for Allah loveth those who judge in equity.

Use but do not abuse

Several times in the Qur'an, humans are invited to make use of the nourishing goods that Allah has placed on earth for them, but abuse—particularly through extravagance and excess—is strictly forbidden. Sometimes these principles are stated in one breath, so to speak. Sometimes they are stated separately. But the message is the same, as the following verse indicates:

007.031. O children of Adam! . . . eat and drink: but waste not by excess for Allah loveth not the wasters.

There are as many invitations to partake of nature as provided for humans and for other creatures of the earth as there are for the avoidance of wasteful extravagance. Time and again, Allah reminds us that He loveth not wasters.

006.141. It is He who produceth gardens with trellises and without and dates and tilth with produce of all kinds and olives and pomegranates

similar [in kind] and different [in variety]: eat of their fruit in their season
but render the dues that are proper on the day that the harvest is gathered.
But waste not by excess: for Allah loveth not the wasters.

Fitra

The last principle that we bring forth in our examination of the Qur'anic
underpinnings of conservation is that of fitra. Fitra can be taken as perhaps the most direct injunction by Allah to humans to conserve the environment and not to change the balance of His creation. This is specifically
contained in the verse below:

> 030.030. So set thou thy face steadily and truly to the Faith: [Establish]
> Allah's handiwork according to the pattern on which He has made
> mankind: no change [let there be] in the work [wrought] by Allah: that is
> the standard Religion: but most among mankind understand not.

Thus, Islam teaches that humanity is an integral part of the environment; it is part of the creation of Almighty God. We remain deeply locked
into the natural domain despite the fact that there is talk of bringing the
environment to the people as though we were independent of it.

The power given to us by God is seen in Islam to be limited by the
responsibilities we bear, not only toward God and other men and
women, but also toward the rest of creation.

Seyyed Hossein Nasr says: "The Divine Law (al shariah) is explicit
in extending the religious duties of man to the natural order and the
environment."[3]

Conclusion

As we indicated at the beginning, there are a number of Qur'anic principles that, taken separately, do not have an obvious connection with
conservation. But taken in their totality, they state in clear terms that
Allah, the One True God, is the Universal God and the Creator of the
Universe and, indeed, the Owner of the Universe. To Him belong all the
animate and inanimate objects, all of whom should or do submit themselves to Him. Allah, in His Wisdom, appointed us, the creatures that He
has conferred with the faculty of reason and with free will, to be His vice
regents on earth. And while Allah has invited us to partake of the fruits
of the earth for our rightful nourishment and enjoyment, He has also

---

3. S. H. Nasr, *The Need for a Sacred Science* (London: Curzon Press, 1990).

directed us not to waste that which Allah has provided for us—for He loveth not wasters. Furthermore, Allah has also ordered us to administer his responsibilities with Justice. Above all, humanity should conserve the balance of Allah's creation on Earth. By virtue of our intelligence, we (when we believe in the One Universal Allah, the Creator of the Universe) are the only creation of Allah to be entrusted with the overall responsibility of maintaining planet Earth in the overall balanced ecology that we found. If biologists believe that humans are the greatest agent of ecological change on the surface of the earth, is it not they who, drawn from the brink, will—for their own good—abandon Mammon and listen to the prescriptions of God on the conservation of their environment and the environment of all the creatures on earth? The Islamic answer to this question is decisively in the affirmative.

13

Jainism

This statement was prepared on behalf of the Institute of Jainology by its president, Dr. L. M. Singhvi. The Institute of Jainology is the main body bringing together the three distinct traditions of the Jains.

Jainism is one of the oldest living religions. The term Jain means "follower of the Jinas." The Jinas, or spiritual victors, are human teachers who attained omniscience. They are also called Tirthankaras (ford-makers), those who help others escape the cycle of birth and death. The twenty-fourth Tirthankara, called Mahavira, was born in 599 B.C. At the age of 30, he left home on a spiritual quest, and after 12 years of trials and austerities, he attained omniscience. Eleven men became his ganadharas, or chief disciples. At 72 Mahavira died and attained nirvana, that blissful state beyond life and death. Mahavira was not the founder of a new religion. He consolidated the faith by drawing together the teachings of the previous Tirthankaras, particularly those of his immediate predecessor, Parsva, who lived about 250 years earlier at Varnasi.

Initially the followers of Jainism lived throughout the Ganges Valley in India. Around 250 B.C., most Jains migrated to the city of Mathura on the Yamuna River. Later, many traveled west to Rajasthan and Gujarat and south to Maharashtra and Karnataka, where Jainism rapidly grew in popularity. The Jain population throughout the world is less than 10 million, of which about 100,000 have settled overseas in North America, the United Kingdom, Kenya, Belgium, Singapore, Hong Kong, and Japan.

Jain practices

Jains believe that to attain the higher stages of personal development, lay people must adhere to the three jewels (ratna-traya), namely, enlightened worldview, true knowledge, and conduct based on enlightened worldview and true knowledge. They must endeavor to fulfil the anu-vratas (small vows). There are five such vows.

Ahimsa (nonviolence)

This is the fundamental vow and runs through the Jain tradition like a golden thread. It involves avoidance of violence in any form through word or deed, not only to human beings but also to all nature. It means reverence for life in every form including plants and animals. Jains prac-tice the principle of compassion for all living beings (Jiva-daya) at every step in daily life. Jains are vegetarians.

Satya (truthfulness)

"Tirthankara Mahavira" (Truth is God) said Sachham Bhagwam.

Asteya (not stealing)

This is the principle of not taking what belongs to another. It means avoidance of greed and exploitation.

Brahmacharya (chastity)

This means practicing restraint and avoiding sexual promiscuity.

Aparigraha (non-materialism)

For lay Jains, this means limiting their acquisition of material goods and contributing one's wealth and time to humanitarian charities and phil-anthropic causes.

Jain beliefs

Anekantavada (non-one-sidedness)

This philosophy states that no single perspective on any issue contains the whole truth. It emphasizes the concept of universal interdependence and specifically recommends that one should take into account the view-points of other species, other communities and nations, and other human beings.

Loka (the universe)

Space is infinite but only a finite portion is occupied by what is known as the universe. Everything within the universe, whether sentient (jiva) or insentient (ajiva), is eternal, although the forms that a thing may take are transient. Jains preach and practice the principle of the duty of every human being to promote universal well-being (sarva-mangalya).

Jiva (soul)

All living beings have an individual soul (jiva) which occupies the body, a conglomerate of atoms. At the time of death, the soul leaves the body and immediately takes birth in another. Attaining nirvana and thereby terminating this cycle of birth and death is the goal of Jain practice.

Ajiva (non-soul)

Ajiva is everything in the universe that is insentient, including matter, the media of motion and rest, time and space.

Karma

Karma is understood as a form of subtle matter that adheres to the soul as a result of its actions of body, speech, and mind. This accumulated karma is the cause of the soul's bondage in the cycle of birth and death.

Moksha or nirvana (eternal liberation through enlightenment)

The ultimate aim of life is to emancipate the soul from the cycle of birth and death. This is done by exhausting all bound karmas and preventing further accumulation. To achieve moksha, it is necessary to have enlightened worldview, knowledge, and conduct.

Jainism is fundamentally a religion of ecology and has turned ecology into a religion. It has enabled Jains to create an environment-friendly value system and code of conduct. Because of the insistence on rationality in the Jain tradition, Jains are always ready and willing to look positively and with enthusiasm upon environmental causes. In India and abroad, they are in the forefront of bringing greater awareness and putting into practice their cardinal principles on ecology. Their programs have been modest and mostly self-funded through volunteers.

14

Judaism

Professor Nahum Rakover, an Orthodox legalist and Torah/Talmud scholar, was appointed by the World Jewish Congress to write this statement.

Consider the work of God; for who can make that straight, which man has made crooked? (Eccles. 7:13)

When God created Adam, he showed him all the trees of the Garden of Eden and said to him: "See my works, how lovely they are, how fine they are. All I have created, I created for you. Take care not to corrupt and destroy my universe, for if you destroy it, no one will come after you to put it right." (Ecclesiastes Rabbah 7)

The present paper is concerned with the vast and complex problem of protecting our natural environment from pollution and destruction, so that we can live in God's world while enjoying its beauty and deriving from it the maximum physical and spiritual benefit.

In Jewish sources, the rationale for humanity's obligation to protect nature may be found in the biblical expression, "For the earth is Mine" (Lev. 25:23). The Bible informs us that the Earth is not subject to man's absolute ownership, but is rather given to us "to use and protect" (Gen. 2:15).

From biblical sources that refer to our "dominion" over nature, it would appear as though we were granted unlimited control of this world, as we find in Genesis 1:26:

And God said, "Let us make man in our image, after our likeness; and let them have dominion over the fish of the sea, and over the fowl of the air, and over the cattle and over all the earth, and over every creeping thing that creeps upon the earth."

And again in Genesis 1:28:

And God blessed [Adam and Eve]: "Be fruitful, and multiply, and fill the earth and subdue it; and have dominion over the fish of the sea, and over the fowl of the air, and over every living thing that creeps upon the earth."

Rav Kook[1] has an insightful understanding of the idea:

There can be no doubt to any enlightened or thoughtful person, that the "dominion" mentioned in the Bible in the phrase, "and have dominion over the fish of the sea, and over the fowl of the air, and over every living thing that creeps upon the earth," is not the dominion of a tyrant who deals harshly with his people and servants in order to achieve his own personal desires and whims. It would be unthinkable to legislate so repugnant a subjugation and have it forever engraved upon the world of God, who is good to all and whose mercy extends to all He has created, as is written, "the earth is founded upon mercy" (Ps. 89:3).[2]

Three things that grant man tranquility

The Sages of the Talmud gave expression to the environment's effect on the human spirit in their statement:

Three things restore a man's consciousness: [beautiful] sounds, sights, and smells. Three things enlarge a man's spirit: a beautiful dwelling, a beautiful wife, and beautiful clothes.[3]

The Sages of the Talmud also noted that the environment undergoes more damage in large cities than in small towns. In explaining a law of the Mishnah,[4] that a spouse may not compel his mate to move from a village to a large city, the Talmud cites the reasoning of R. Yosi ben Hanina,[5] "Life is more difficult in the city." Rashi explains:[6]

---

1. R. Avraham Yitzhak haKohen Kook (1865–1935) was the first chief rabbi of Palestine. Philosopher, scholar, legal authority, and mystic, he was one of the outstanding Jewish personalities of recent generations.

2. "Hazon haTzimhonut vehaShalom, Afikim baNegev II," in *Lahai Ro'i*, ed. Yohanan Fried and Avraham Riger (Jerusalem, 1961), 207.

3. Berakhot 57b.

4. Mishnah Ketubot 13:10.

5. Ketubot 110b.

6. Rashi, ad loc., s.v. Yeshivat.

Because so many live there, and they crowd their houses together, and there is no air, whereas in villages there are gardens and orchards close to the homes, and the air is good.[7]

One who threw stones into the public domain

We learn of the obligation of the individual to protect the public domain from a story included in the Tosefta:

It happened that a certain person was removing stones from his ground onto public ground when a pious man found him and said, "Fool, why do you remove stones from ground which is not yours to ground which is yours?" The man laughed at him. Some time later he was compelled to sell his field, and when he was walking on that public ground, he stumbled over the stones he had thrown there. He then said, "How well did that pious man say to me, Why do you remove stones from ground which is not yours to ground which is yours?"[8]

In other words, the terms "private domain" and "public domain" are not necessarily identical to the concepts "mine" and "not mine." What was once my private domain might one day not be mine, while the public domain will always remain my domain.

Protection of the environment and the love of man

In addition to the rules governing man's relations with his fellow man, which are based upon the biblical imperative "Love your neighbor as yourself" (Lev. 19:18), norms were established for man's treatment of plants, animals,[9] and even the inanimate elements of nature.

When approaching the subject of environmental protection, we must be careful to maintain the proper balance between protection of the environment and protection of humanity. The proper balance in this context is certainly not one of equality between man and nature. The relationship between man and nature is one of ownership—albeit limited. In our enthusiasm for protecting the environment, we must not forget man's

---

7. R. Yosi ben Hanina's opinion was codified as law: Maimonides, M. T., Ishut 13:17. See also Shul. Ar. Even haEzer 75:1.

8. Tosefta Baba Kama 2:10.

9. On the attitude to animals, see Nahum Rakover, Hagannat haHai (Tzed Hayyot), monograph no. 40 of Sidrat Mehkarim uSekirot baMishpat haIvri (Jerusalem, 1976).

interests or his role in the scheme of creation. Love of nature may not take precedence over love of humanity. We must avoid at all costs the error of those who were known as lovers of animals yet perpetrated the worst crimes imaginable against their fellow men.

The proper balance must also be maintained between individual interests and the interest of the public. Sometimes an individual's act may harm the community, as when a person builds a factory that pollutes the environment with industrial waste. Sometimes, however, it is the community that is interested in a factory although it constitutes a serious infringement upon an individual's ability to enjoy his own home and surroundings.

When discussing the quality of the environment, we must remember that the environment also comprises the people living in it—individuals and community. Protection of the environment, by itself, cannot solve conflicts of interest, though it can extend the range of factors considered when seeking solutions to problems. Solutions must, in the final analysis, be based upon economic, social, and moral considerations.

In our survey, we examine Jewish sources that relate to our topic. We shall mention the limitations imposed on acts that do harm to nature, one's neighbors, and society at large.

A number of the subjects we investigate are rooted in the laws governing relations among neighbors and the laws of torts. These laws are numerous and complex, and a comprehensive discussion of them all is far beyond the scope of the present survey. We shall, however, attempt to cover briefly a number of the guiding principles in these areas. And even if we do not find solutions for all the problems raised, we hope that we can at least refine the questions and pose challenges for further analysis of the issues.

Protecting nature

Man and his environment

I recall the early days, from 1905 onward, when it was granted me by the grace of the blessed Lord to go up to the holy land, and I came to Jaffa. There I first went to visit our great master R. Abraham Isaac Kook (of blessed memory), who received me with good cheer, as it was his hallowed custom to receive everyone. We chatted together on themes of Torah study. After the afternoon service, he went out, as was his custom, to stroll a bit in the fields and gather his thoughts; and I went along. On the way, I plucked some branch or flower. Our great master was taken aback; and then he told me gently, "Believe me. In all my days I have taken care never to pluck a blade of grass or flower needlessly, when it had the ability to grow or blossom. You know the teaching of the Sages that there is not a single blade of grass below, here on earth, which does not have a heavenly force telling it Grow! Every sprout and leaf of grass says something, conveys some meaning. Every stone whispers some inner, hidden message in the silence. Every creation utters its song (in praise of the Creator)." Those words, spoken from a pure and holy heart, engraved themselves deeply on my heart. From that time on, I began to feel a strong sense of compassion for everything. (R. Aryeh Levine[10])

Rav Kook's attitude toward each individual plant and to the creation in general is based upon a comprehensive philosophical approach to man's relationship with nature. This position was well articulated by the noted mystic R. Moshe Cordovero[11] in his work *Tomer Devorah:*

One's mercy must extend to all the oppressed. One must not embarrass or destroy them, for the higher wisdom is spread over all that was created: inanimate, vegetable, animal, and human. For this reason were we warned against desecrating food stuffs . . . and in the same way, one must not desecrate anything, for all was created by His wisdom—nor should one uproot a plant, unless there is a need, or kill an animal unless there is a need.[12]

The sabbatical year

The idea of conservation may be found in the biblical institution of the sabbatical year (Lev. 25:1–5):

And the Lord spoke unto Moses on Mount Sinai, saying: Speak unto the children of Israel, and say unto them: When you come into the land which I give you, then shall the land keep a sabbath unto the Lord. Six years shall you sow your field, and six years shall you prune your vineyard, and gather in the produce thereof. But in the seventh year shall be a sabbath of solemn rest for the land, a sabbath unto the Lord; you shall neither sow your field nor prune your vineyard.

That which grows of itself of your harvest you shall not reap, and the grapes of your undressed vine you shall not gather; it shall be a year of solemn rest for the land.[13]

---

10. R. Aryeh Levine was known as the "prisoners' rabbi." The passage appears in Simcha Raz, *A Tzadik in Our Times*, trans. Charles Wengrov (Jerusalem, 1976), 108–109.

11. R. Moshe Cordovero (1522–1570) was the leading kabbalist of Safed in the period preceding R. Yitzhak Luria.

12. Tomer Devorah 3, ad fin.

13. See also Lev. 25:6–7 and Exod. 23:10–11.

Maimonides,[14] in his *Guide of the Perplexed*, suggests a reason for the sabbatical year:

> With regard to all the commandments that we have enumerated in Laws concerning the Sabbatical year and the Jubilee, some of them are meant to lead to pity and help for all men—as the text has it: "That the poor of the people may eat; and what they leave, the beasts of the field shall eat . . ." (Exod. 23:11)—and are meant to make the earth more fertile and stronger through letting it fallow.[15]

In other words, one of the goals of ceasing all agricultural activity is to improve and strengthen the land.

Another reason for the sabbatical year which emphasizes our relationship with our environment is suggested by the author of Sefer haHinnukh in his explanation of the obligation to declare all produce ownerless (so that anyone may enter any field and take from its produce) during the sabbatical year.[16]

To the reasons for the sabbatical year, Rav Kook adds restoration of the proper balance among humanity, God, and nature. In the sabbatical year, according to Rav Kook:

> man returns to the freshness of his nature, to the point where there is no need to heal his illnesses, most of which result from destruction of the balance of life as it departs ever further from the purity of spiritual and material nature. (Introduction to Shabbat haAretz, 8–9)

To establish in our hearts and make a strong impression on our thoughts that the world was created as a new entity out of nothing, "that in six days God made the heaven and the earth" (Exod. 20:11);

> . . . and on the seventh day, when He created nothing, he decreed rest for Himself . . . And, therefore, the Holy One commanded [us] to declare all produce of the earth ownerless during this [sabbatical] year in addition to cessation of agricultural work, so that man will remember that the earth which yields its produce for him each year, does not do so on its own strength or of itself, but rather there is one who is Master over the land

---

14. Maimonides, R. Moshe ben Maimon (1135–1204), was born in Cordoba, Spain. He was the most distinguished Jewish authority of the Middle Ages.

15. Maimonides, *The Guide of the Perplexed,* trans. Shlomo Pines (Chicago: University of Chicago Press, 1963), III:39.

16. Sefer haHinnukh, commandment 84 (ed. Chavel, commandment 69). Cf. Sefer haHinnukh on the Jubilee Year, commandment 330 (ed. Chavel, commandment 326): 'God wished to teach His people that all belongs to Him, that ultimately all things are returned to the one to whom God wished to give them at the outset. For the world is His, as is written "(Ex. 19:5) . . . for all the earth is Mine."

and its owners, and when He wishes, He commands that the produce be ownerless.

It is worth noting that the institution of the sabbatical year is practiced into modern times within observant circles; the last sabbatical observed was in 1993–94 (corresponding to the Hebrew calendar year 5754).

Altering creation

In addition to refraining from overexploitation of the earth's resources, we must also be mindful of preserving the natural balance of creation. This is the approach taken by R. Avraham ibn Ezra[17] in his explanation of the biblical prohibition against mixing species. In Leviticus (19:19) we find:

> You shall keep my statutes. You shall not let your cattle gender with a diverse kind; you shall not sow your field with two kinds of seed; neither shall there come upon you a garment of two kinds of stuff mingled together.

One aspect of preventing changes in the creation finds expression in the effort to avoid causing the extinction of any animal. The presumption that everything that was created was created for some purpose denies us the possibility of eliminating from the world any species. So writes Nahmanides concerning the prohibition of mixing species:[18]

> The reason for the prohibition against mixing species is that God created all the species of the earth . . . and gave them the power to reproduce so that their species could exist forever, for as long as He wishes the world to exist, and He created for each one the capacity to reproduce its own species and not change it, forever. . . . And this is the reason for sexual reproduction among animals, to maintain the species; so too among humans, it is for the purpose of being fruitful and multiplying.[19]

---

17. R. Avraham ibn Ezra (ca. 1089–1164) was a biblical commentator, poet, philosopher, and physician. He lived in Spain.

18. Nahmanides, Lev. 19:19.

19. See also Nahmanides, Tatyag Mitzvot haYotzim meAseret haDibrot, in *Kitvei haRamban*, ed. Chaim Chavel, vol. 2, 544.

T. J. Kilayim 1:7 on Lev. 19:19: "You shall keep my laws—the [natural] laws I have established in my world." Cf. T. B. Kiddushin 39a, and Sanhedrin 60a. But see Gen. 1:26, "and let them have dominion over the fish of the sea"; and Gen. 1:28, and the comments of Nahmanides, ad loc., cited above, text to notes 3 and 5.

See also Sefer haHinnukh, commandment 244 (ed. Chavel, commandment 249), concerning the prohibition of breeding one species with another; and commandment 245 (ed. Chavel, commandment 250), concerning the prohibition of planting different species of seeds together.

Prohibition of wasteful destruction

An additional expression of our obligation to preserve our natural environment may be found in the commandment against wasteful destruction, bal tash'hit. In general, the commandment prohibits the destruction of anything from which humans may benefit. It applies to the destruction of animals, plants, and even inanimate objects.[20]

Instructive remarks are found in Sefer haHinnukh's discussion of the prohibition against cutting down fruit-bearing trees. The discussion opens with a discourse on the scope of the commandment:

> We have been prevented from cutting down trees when we lay siege to a city in order to press and bring pain to the hearts of its residents, as is said, "you shall not destroy the trees thereof . . . and you shall not cut them down" (Deut. 20:19). Included in this prohibition is destruction of every type, such as burning or tearing a garment, or breaking a vessel for no reason.[21]

The author of Sefer haHinnukh then goes on to explain the reason for the prohibition:

> It is known that this commandment is meant to teach us to love the good and the useful and cling to them, and in this way goodness will cling to us, and we will avoid all that is bad and decadent. And this is the way of the pious: They love peace and rejoice in the good fortune of others, and bring everyone near to the Torah, and do not waste even a mustard seed, and they are pained by all destruction and waste that they see. And they save anything they can from destruction with all their might. But the wicked are different. They are the allies of those who destroy, they rejoice in destruction of the world and they destroy themselves: "with the kind of measure a man measures, so shall he be measured . . ." (Mishnah Sotah 1:7)

The source of the prohibition against wasteful destruction is the biblical prohibition of cutting down fruit-bearing trees, which will be discussed below. The prohibition of wasteful destruction, however, is more comprehensive than the prohibition of destroying fruit-bearing trees, and it extends to anything that has use. In other words, the prohibition includes the destruction of manmade objects, and is not restricted to the preservation of nature.

---

20. See *Encyclopedia Talmudit*, s.v. Bal tash'hit; Nahum Rakover, *A Bibliography of Jewish Law—Otzar haMishpat* (Jerusalem: Harry Fischel Institute for Research in Jewish Law, 1975), s.v. Bal tash'hit, vol. 1, 285, and vol. 2, 278.

21. Sefer haHinnukh, commandment 529 (ed. Chavel, commandment 530).

In the book of Deuteronomy (20:19), among the laws concerning the waging of war, we find:

> When you shall besiege a city a long time, in making war against it to take it, you shall not destroy the trees thereof by wielding an axe against them; for you may eat of them, but you shall not cut them down; for is the tree of the field man, that it should be besieged by you?

The Bible thus warns that even in time of war, it is forbidden to destroy fruit-bearing trees.

The author[22] of haKetav vehaKabbalah explains the prohibition:[23]

> It is not proper to use some created thing for a purpose diametrically opposed to the purpose for which it was created, as has been stated[24] concerning Exodus 20:22: "for if you lift up your sword to it, you have profaned it"—the altar was created to prolong the life of man, and iron was created to shorten the life of man; thus it is not fitting that something which shortens man's life be used upon that which lengthens it. So too a tree, which was created to make fruit to nourish men and animals, should have nothing done to it that destroys man.

The relationship of God, man, and nature is depicted in the biblical expression, "For man is a tree of the field."[25] Various interpretations have been given to this relationship: Even plants are subject to divine Providence; both man and the tree are God's creatures. Sifrei asserts, "This shows that man's living comes from trees."[26]

The Sages also compared the death of the tree to the departure of man's soul from his body:[27]

> There are five sounds that go from one end of the world to the other, though they are inaudible. When people cut down the wood of a tree that yields fruit, its cry goes from one end of the world to the other, and the sound is inaudible. . . . When the soul departs from the body, the cry goes forth from one end of the world to the other, and the sound is inaudible.[28]

---

22. R. Ya'akov Tzvi Mecklenberg (d. 1865), head of the rabbinic court of Koenigsberg.

23. haKetav vehaKabbalah, Deut. 20:19.

24. Mekhilta, Exod. 2:22; Rashi on the same verse.

25. Read as a statement rather than as a question.

26. Sifrei (ed. Finkelstein), 203.

27. Pirkei Rabbi Eliezer 34; see also commentary of R. David Luria, ad loc.

28. Just as there are sounds inaudible to human beings because of their high frequency, so the Sages know of additional sounds that humans are incapable of hearing.

On the basis of this passage, R. Menahem Recanati[29] comments that when we wreak destruction in the material world, destruction is wreaked in the metaphysical world as well and that this is what was meant by "For man is a tree of the field."[30]

Polluting the environment: Smoking

Smoking constitutes a serious environmental pollutant and danger to health. Public awareness of this problem has led to legislation against smoking in public places.[31]

Jewish legal authorities have considered whether it is prohibited to smoke in places where the smoke might bother others. One authority who absolutely prohibits smoking in public places is R. Moshe Feinstein.[32] It is his opinion that even if smoking were irritating only to those who are hypersensitive, it would nevertheless be prohibited to smoke in public places.[33] Precedent for this holding is the talmudic case of R. Yosef, who was hypersensitive to noise. If it is possible to restrain particular actions on the basis of hypersensitivity, R. Feinstein reasons, certainly it is possible to do so where there is pain or injury. Thus, where smoking is harmful to others, it is certainly prohibited.[34]

Beauty

> On seeing creatures that are beautiful or exceptionally well-formed or goodly trees, one says, "Blessed are You, O Lord our God, King of the universe who has such as these in His world." If one goes out into the fields or gardens during the month of Nisan [i.e., the spring] and sees the trees

---

29. R. Menahem Recanati was an early kabbalist active in Italy at the end of the thirteenth century and the beginning of the fourteenth century.

30. Commentary of Recanati, Shofetim. See also Yalkut meAm Lo'ez, Deut. 17.

31. In 1983, the Israeli Knesset enacted the Restriction of Smoking in Public Places Law, which was supplemented in 1994 by an executive order signed by the minister of health (Kovetz Takkanot, 21 July 1994, 1197–98). The executive order confines smoking in the workplace to specially designated areas where there are no nonsmokers, where there is adequate ventilation, and where smoking does not cause a nuisance to other parts of the workplace.

32. R. Moshe Feinstein (1895–1986) was considered the spiritual leader of American Orthodoxy and American Jewry's leading authority on Jewish law in recent years.

33. See Resp. Iggerot Moshe, Hoshen Mishpat II:18.

34. See M. Halperin, "haIshun—Sekirah Hilkhatit," Asia, V (1986), 238–247; A. S. Avraham, Nishmat Avraham, Hoshen Mishpat 155:2; Dov Ettinger, Pe' er Tahat Efer—haIshun biYemei Hol uveYamim Tovim leOr haHalakhah (Jerusalem, 1989).

budding and the flowers in bloom, he says, "Blessed are You, O Lord our God, King of the universe, who has made Your world lacking in nought and created therein beautiful creatures and goodly trees for the benefit of mankind."[35]

Aesthetic beauty appears in Jewish sources not only as a value worthy of fostering in the life of the individual and the community, but also as the basis for a variety of legal obligations. The obligations derive from biblical regulations and from rabbinic legislation.

In the Pentateuch (Num. 35:2–5),[36] we find instructions regarding city planning, which required designation of open spaces free of all obstruction. Rashi describes the purpose of the open strip as being "for the beautification of the city, that it have air."[37]

Later rabbinical legislation expanded the applicability of this rule to include cities other than those mentioned in the Bible.[38]

Current activities

The ideas of environmental protection and land conservation in the Jewish faith currently find application on a number of levels.

In Israel, the year 1994 was declared the "Year of the Environment." One of the many results of this declaration was that the environment was selected as the central theme of the Israeli educational system.

In honor of the Year of the Environment, the book *Environment Reflections and Perspectives in Jewish Sources* was published. The book analyzes the ideas of our relation to the environment, as well as the vast legislative material in this area, from Scripture, the Mishnah, and Talmud (second through fifth centuries) through the well-known codifiers, such as Maimonides and the Shulhan Arukh, and the rich responsa literature. The book also traces how principles of environmental protection were given expression in ordinances passed in Jerusalem's new neighborhoods constructed outside the city walls in the late nineteenth and early twentieth centuries.

Booklets on the Jewish sources concerning environmental protection were also prepared for use in the school system.

The Israeli legislature, the Knesset, has enacted laws in such relevant areas as air and noise pollution, water pollution, recycling of waste, dangerous substances, protection of wildlife and vegetation,

---

35. Maimonides, M. T., Berakhot 10:13.

36. See also Lev. 25:34.

37. Rashi, Sotah 27b, s.v. Migrash. Cf. Rashi's comments on Num. 35:2.

38. Maimonides, M. T., Shemitah veYovel 13:1–2, 4–5.

and establishment of nature preserves. It is the hope of the Jewish people that these activities further strengthen the awareness of environmental issues in Israel and throughout the world.

Summary

Humanity and creation

The philosophical basis for our relationship with our environment in general and the plant kingdom in particular was emphasized in early sources, in the Midrash, and in various philosophical works. The classic Jewish attitude to nature is a direct consequence of the belief that the entire universe is the work of the Creator. Love of God was taken in the broadest sense to include love of all His creations: the inanimate, plants, animals, and human beings. Nature in all its beauty is understood as having been created for us, and it is, therefore, wrong for us to spoil it. Our connection to nature can restore us to our original character, to a natural state of happiness and joy.

Balancing interests

Protecting the environment involves protection of the natural balance, which includes, among other factors, the balance between us and the creation. But balance in this context does not mean equality. Balance may entail granting preference to us and our welfare, both physical and spiritual, and spiritual welfare may even take precedence over physical welfare. Conflicts of interest must be resolved by a careful weighing of values, a process that may sometimes result in absolute rejection of one value in favor of another. Nevertheless, in spite of our preferred status, preservation of the environment need not necessarily be the value rejected. In some cases, it is our interest that will be rejected in favor of the environment, particularly when the benefit to us is marginal, and damage to the environment is significant.

Humanity's ownership is not absolute

Our control over the world is restricted. "For the earth is Mine" (Lev. 25:23): only the Creator may be considered to enjoy absolute ownership of His creation. We are commanded not to spoil the creation, but rather to improve and perfect it.

Our rights in property are restricted. We may not use our possessions in ways likely to harm others. Principles were set forth for protecting the public domain, be it those areas "owned" by the public or areas, such as the ozone layer that protects us from the harmful rays of the sun, that belong to no one but serve all.

Attitude toward man

"Love thy neighbor as thyself" (Lev. 19:18), the basis for all Jewish ethics, is applied to protection of the environment in the obligation to exercise care not to harm others, and particularly in the obligation to avoid doing harm to the community. In proper relationships between man and his fellow man, and between man and his environment, the legal and ethical boundaries between "mine" and "not mine" become blurred.

Determining legal principles

In typical fashion, Jewish sources were not satisfied with merely emphasizing "environmental values," but also established concrete legal obligations. Jewish legal sources contain extensive discussion of the environmental issues that concern modern society, and point the way to protection against smoke, odors, pollution of air and water, and damage to the natural landscape.

Legal perspectives

The basic principles of environmental protection, and the actions that flow from these principles, are based upon scripture, and upon the reasons proposed for various commandments. The development of these principles continues in the post-biblical legal discourse of the Mishnah, Talmud, codes, and responses.

In addition to various legal categories—such as torts—with implications for protection of the environment, both biblical law and subsequent legislation contain regulations aimed directly at environmental issues. Some of these restricted the rights of the individual vis-à-vis his environment, while others, on the contrary, extended his rights by permitting use of the public domain for personal needs. Special regulations were enacted for Jerusalem because of that city's unique status.

Extreme forms of nuisance

From the area of torts law, we learn of the serious view taken by the Sages toward damage to the environment.

Certain types of nuisance, such as smoke, foul odors, and noise, were classified as extreme, and those responsible for them were not permitted to claim "unchallenged practice" in their defense. In such instances, the injured party's failure to protest does not establish the perpetrator's right to continue this offensive practice. Since the damage in these cases is to the injured party—not to the property—and causes suffering, the law presumes that one never waives one's right to restrain the perpetrator. A similar principle operates for aesthetic values of the city, where residents do not have the power to waive enforcement of ordinances protecting aesthetic standards.

A person can be held responsible not only for causing direct damage to the environment, but also for creating circumstances that lead to damage. So, for instance, even if a person makes no noise himself, but rather creates a situation that causes noise to be produced, he can be restrained.

Even where compensation cannot be had, because the damage is indirect, the person who creates the circumstances that cause the damage can be compelled to desist.

Various activities and facilities must be located so as to prevent their doing damage to their surroundings. The distances specified in the Mishnah apply to conditions that pertained at the time of that work's compilation. As conditions change, however, distances must be adjusted accordingly.

Flexibility in establishing norms

Simple solutions do not exist for all problems. Just as in family law, where it is difficult to give precise definition to the types of behavior that ought to result from the relationship of love and respect between man and wife, patterns of behavior based upon love of nature and the creation cannot be readily translated into fixed, inflexible norms. Nevertheless, even where there is no set answer, the Sages developed criteria that can be applied to new and changing situations. Some questions will turn on the relative importance given to the welfare of the individual or the community on the one hand and environmental values on the other.

In mediating among competing values, the relative weight that should be assigned to the society's attitude to nature remains uncertain. It would seem important to ensure that there is not too great a gap between the attitude of the society and the obligations imposed by law, lest the demands be greater than the population can bear.

In our own time, the number of threats to the environment has increased greatly as a result of the growth of large urban centers and the development of industry. Smoke, industrial waste, untreated sewage, dumping sites in close proximity to residential areas, damage to the ozone layer, and various other ecological evils represent a real danger not only to the environment and the quality of life, but to life itself.

Today, the danger to the environment is many times greater than at any other time in history. Thus the increasing importance of the Jewish values and the approaches contained in Jewish legal sources. If the proper course is followed, we will not forfeit our opportunity to live a life of comfort in our environment, nor will the environment be uncomfortable with us.

Harmony in four parts

Rabbi Avraham Yitzhak haKohen Kook wrote as follows:

> One man sings the song of his own soul, for it is there that his satisfaction is complete.
>
> Another sings the song of his people, transcending the bounds of his own individual soul . . . cleaving with tender love to the Jewish people, singing her songs with her. . . .
>
> A third man's soul expands beyond the Jewish people to sing the song of man, his spirit embraces all humanity, majestic reflection of God. . . .
>
> And a fourth is transported still higher, uniting with the entire universe, with all creatures, and all worlds, with all of these does he sing. . . . [39]

---

39. Orot haKodesh II, 444.

15
Shintoism

This statement was prepared by the Jinja Honcho, the representative body of all Shinto Shrines in Japan.

According to Kojiki, which is the oldest literature that we presently have, in the beginning of the universe there appeared various Kami (deities) from the chaos. A pair of male and female deities appeared at the end and gave birth first to islands, their natural environment, and then to several more deities who became ancestors of the Japanese.

The ancient Japanese considered that all things of this world have their own spirituality, as they were born from the divine couple. Therefore, the relationship between the natural environment of this world and people is that of blood kin, like the bond between brother and sister.

An agricultural society based on rice cultivation like that of Japan cannot exist without unification and harmony among all things on this earth: mountains, rivers, the sun, rain, animals, and plants, not to mention cooperation among people. So, it was natural that people developed the idea that they could make their society flourish only when they worked together, fully performing their own role, but at the same time, helping and supporting each other. This gave rise to the spirit of revering various Kami, the land, nature, people, and, on top of that, the spirit of appreciation of harmony among all these aspects of nature.

Kami of Shinto

Shinto regards that the land, its nature, and all creatures including humans are children of Kami. Accordingly, all things existing on this earth have the possibility of becoming Kami. Nevertheless, revered status as Kami is limited to those that live quite extraordinary lives beyond human wisdom or power and that have a profound influence, for good or ill, on human beings. As to natural elements or phenomena that have such enormous power, there exist Kami of Rain, Kami of River, Kami of Thunder, Kami of Wind, Kami of Mountain, Kami of Ocean. All these Kami are involved in the life of a rice-cultivating agricultural society.

Speaking of the reverence toward Kami of Mountain, it started with people's awareness of mountains as an important source of water for rice cultivation. Then, people came to regard the mountain itself as a sacred object. This mountain faith prepared the way not only for the preservation of mountain forests but also for conservation of the cycle of the ecosystem, given the fact that mountain forests supply rich nutrition to seas through rivers and support good fishing.

In ancient times, reverence toward a holy mountain was expressed by paying respect directly to the mountain itself. Nowadays, Shinto has a building, or a compound of buildings, where Kami spirit dwells permanently, and people worship by performing matsuri, a festival to offer prayers to Kami, in these buildings.

There are many kinds of matsuri performed in each locality throughout the year. Large or small, these matsuri are mostly based on the agricultural cycle. Two of the most important festivals each year are the spring festival called Kinensai, a festival to pray for a rich harvest, and the autumn festival called Niinamesai, a festival to offer thanks for the successful harvest. People of each locality have been carrying out these festivals every year since ancient times. In this sense, it can be said that Shinto consists of reverence and gratitude to the land, its nature, and the life that these natural elements give to human beings.

With the reverence of Kami, Shinto spontaneously developed through the way of life of the ancient Japanese. It has neither written dogma nor a teaching book, but people revere numerous deities who are figuratively described as "8 million different deities." A deity with a female form, Amaterasu Ohmikami, is revered most highly among them, but the idea of one absolute god or a hierarchy among numerous Kami has never existed, and still does not. Yet, each Kami has an individual character to which people offer their worship, believing in that as the virtue of each Kami.

Suggestions from Shinto

Shinto regards the land and its environment as children of Kami. In other words, Shinto sees nature as the divinity itself. These days, people often say, "Be gentle to nature" or "Be gentle to the earth." But these expressions sound somehow like the fault of putting the cart before the horse. We feel it is humanity's arrogance. It seems that humans can dominate nature as the master and ultimately "repair" nature, using technical-scientific means. But Kami is the origin of all lives, and the life of all things is deeply connected to Kami. This leads to an awareness of the sacredness of life and an appreciation for life given by Kami.

From ancient times, Japanese have faced nature and invisible existence with awe and appreciation. And they used to have a principle "to return the thing given to the human as a gift of nature to its original place." Until the Edo era (1603–1867) this circulation system of Japanese society functioned very well. After that, with the development of modern industry, the level of Japanese life was elevated in material terms, and now people enjoy lives free of want. But in fact, the Japanese spirituality inherited from the ancient ancestors has been gradually lost or hidden somewhere deep in our consciousness. It might not be an exaggeration if we said that not only environmental problems but also all problems of modern society have been caused by lack of the awe, reverence, and appreciation for nature that ancient people used to have and taught us.

Environmental issues, after all, depend on our self-awareness of the problems and our determination to take responsibility. We often say that things look different depending upon one's viewpoint. So, Shinto suggests that we should shift our point of view and look at our environment with the spirit of "reverence and gratitude," that is, with the spirit of parental care for children or with the spirit of brotherhood. And if we can extend this spirit to our neighbors, to our society members, to our country members, to peoples of the world, and to nature, too, transcending differences of thought, ethics, and religion, then this spirit will serve to foster criteria and morals indispensable for keeping our human life healthy.

16
Sikhism

This statement was compiled by Sri Akhal Takhat Sahib under the guidance of Sri Singh Sahib Manjit Singh, the Jathedar of Anandapur, who is one of the five spiritual and temporal heads of Sikhism, at the request of the World Sikh Council.

"Creating the world, God has made it a place to practice spirituality."
—Guru Granth Sahib (1035)

The Sikh scripture, Guru Granth Sahib, declares that the purpose of human beings is to achieve a blissful state and to be in harmony with the earth and all creation. It seems, however, that humans have drifted away from that ideal. For the earth is today saturated with problems. It is agonizing over the fate of its inhabitants and their future! It is in peril as never before. Its lakes and rivers are being choked, killing its marine life. Its forests are being denuded. A smoky haze envelops the cities of the world. Human beings are exploiting human beings.

There is a sense of crisis in all parts of the world, in various countries and among various peoples. The demands of national economic growth and individual needs and desires are depleting the natural resources of the earth.

There is serious concern that the earth may no longer be a sustainable biosystem. The major crises facing the earth—the social justice crisis and the environmental crisis—together are heading the earth toward a disastrous situation. The social justice crisis is caused by humanity's confrontation with itself and the environmental crisis is caused by humanity's confrontation with nature.

The social justice crisis is that poverty, hunger, disease, exploitation, and injustice are widespread. There are economic wars over resources and markets.

The rights of the poor and the marginal are violated. Women, constituting half the world's population, have their rights abused.

The environmental crisis caused by humanity's exploitation of nature is leading to the depletion of renewable resources, destruction of forests, and overuse of land for agriculture and habitation. Today pollution is contaminating air, land, and water. Smoke from industries, homes, and vehicles is in the air. Industrial waste and consumer trash are affecting streams and rivers, ponds and lakes. Much of the waste is a product of modern technology; it is not biodegradable and not reusable, and its long-term consequences are unknown. The viability of many animal and plant species, and possibly that of the human species itself, is at stake.

This crisis cries out for an immediate and urgent solution. The crisis requires going back to the basic question of the purpose of human beings in this universe and an understanding of ourselves and God's creation.

We are called to the vision of Guru Nanak, which is a World Society comprising God-conscious human beings who have realized God. To these spiritual beings the earth and the universe are sacred; all life is unity, and their mission is the spiritualization of all.

Guru Nanak laid the foundation of Sikhism in the late fifteenth century. His writings, along with those of other human Gurus who succeeded him and of other spiritual leaders, are included in the scripture known as Guru Granth Sahib. Guru Granth has been the Guru and Divine Master of the Sikhs since 1708, when Guru Gobind Singh declared that there would be no more human Gurus. Guru Nanak and his successors during their lifetime worked toward creating an ideal society that has as its basis spiritual awareness and ethical integrity. The name "Sikh" means disciple or learner of the Truth.

Guru Nanak in his philosophy states that the reality that humans create around themselves is a reflection of their inner state. The current instability of the natural system of the earth—the external environment of human beings—is only a reflection of the instability and pain within humans. The increasing barrenness of the earth's terrain is a reflection of the emptiness within humans.

The solution to problems manifest in our world lies in prayer and in accepting God's hukam. It is difficult to translate certain Sikh concepts accurately. Hukam is one such concept—it may be best described as a combination of God's will, order, and system. With an attitude of humility, and surrender to the Divine Spirit, conscientious human beings can seek to redress the current crises of the environment and of social justice. In the Sikh Way this is done through the guidance of the Guru, who is the Divine Master and messenger of God.

Quoted passages below are taken from the Guru Granth Sahib.

The three postulates

A Sikh theologian, Kapur Singh, explains that Sikhism has three postulates implicit in its teachings:

1. There is no essential duality between spirit and matter.
2. Humans have the capacity to consciously participate in the process of spiritual progression.
3. The highest goal of spiritual progression is harmony with God, while remaining earth-conscious, so that the world itself may be transformed to a spiritual plane of existence.

Unity of spirit and matter and the interconnectedness of all creation

The Sikh view is that spirit and matter are not antagonistic. Guru Nanak declared that the spirit is the only reality and matter is only a form of spirit.

Spirit takes on many forms and names under various conditions:

When I saw truly, I knew that all was primeval.
Nanak, the subtle [spirit] and the gross [material] are, in fact, identical.
(281)
That which is inside a person, the same is outside; nothing else exists. By divine prompting look upon all existence as one and undifferentiated; the same light penetrates all existence. (599)

The chasm between the material and the spiritual is in the minds of humans only. It is a limitation of the human condition that spirit and matter appear as duality, and their unity is not self-evident.

The material universe is God's creation. Its origin was in God and its end is in God, and it operates within God's hukam. Guru Nanak declares that God alone knows the reasons for and the moment of earth's creation. The origin of the universe is unknowable. The act of creation itself, the creation of the primeval atom, was instantaneous, caused by the Will of God.

Further descriptions of the universe and its creation in Sikh scripture are remarkably similar to recent scientific speculation about the universe and its origin. One of the basic hymns in the Sikh scripture, which may be called the "Hymn of the Genesis," describes the indeterminate void before the existence of this universe (appendix 1).

Guru Nanak speaks of innumerable galaxies, of a limitless universe, the boundaries of which are beyond human ability to comprehend. God alone knows the extent of creation (appendix 3).

God created the universe and the world, for reasons best known to Him. And being the results of God's actions, all parts of the universe are holy. God is an all-pervasive being manifest through various elements of creation (appendix 4).

Having created this universe and the world, God directs them. All actions take place within God's hukam. God alone knows how and why. God, however, not only directs this vast and massive theater, but also watches over with care and kindness—the benign, supportive parent!

> Men, trees, pilgrimage places, banks of sacred streams, clouds, fields.
> Islands, spheres, universes, continents, solar systems.
> The sources of creation, egg-born, womb-born, earth-born,
> sweat-born, oceans, mountains and sentient beings.
> He, the Lord, knows their condition, O Nanak.
> Nanak, having created beings, the lord takes care of them all.
> The Creator who created the world, He takes thought of it as well. (466)

The world, like all creation, is a manifestation of God. Every creature in this world, every plant, every form is a manifestation of the Creator. Each is part of God and God is within each element of creation. God is the cause of all and He is the primary connection between all existence.

> The Creator created himself . . .
> And created all creation in which He is manifest.
> You Yourself the bumble-bee, flower, fruit and the tree.
> You Yourself the water, desert, ocean and the pond.
> You Yourself are the big fish, tortoise and the Cause of causes. Your form
> cannot be known. (1016)

In the world God has created he has also provided each species and humans with means of support and nurturing.

In Sikh beliefs, a concern for the environment is part of an integrated approach to life and nature. As all creation has the same origin and end, humans must have consciousness of their place in creation and their relationship with the rest of creation. Humans should conduct themselves through life with love, compassion, and justice. Becoming one and being in harmony with God implies that humans endeavor to live in harmony with all of God's creation.

Spiritual discipline

The second postulate is that humans, practicing a highly disciplined life, while remaining active in the world, are capable of further spiritual progression. It is important that Sikhs retain the primacy of spirit over matter, while it is desirable that they do not deny matter or material existence. It is not required that humans renounce the world. They must maintain their life in the world and uphold all responsibilities in the world. Humans should be renouncers of plenty and maintain a simple life. Further spiritual progress fundamentally starts with an individual conquering himself/herself with the guidance of the Guru (appendix 6).

The emphasis is on mastery over the self and the discovery of the self, not mastery over nature, external forms, and beings. Sikhism teaches against a life of conspicuous, wasteful consumption. The Guru recommends a judicious utilization of material and cultural resources available to humans.

> Then why get attached to what you will leave behind.
> Having wealth, you indulge in pleasures bout,
> From that, tell me, who will bail you out?
> All your houses, horses, elephants and luxurious cars,
> They are just pomp and show, all totally false.

The Gurus taught humans to be aware of and respect the dignity in all life, whether human or not. Such a respect for life can only be fostered where one can first recognize the Divine spark within oneself, see it in others, cherish it, nurture and fulfil it.

> This little shrine of the human body!
> This great opportunity of life!
> The object is to meet the Beloved, thy Master!

Humans have the capability to further their spiritual progression through conscious choice, and it is important to identify the method by which they might do so. The method suggested by Guru Nanak is one of spiritual discipline, meditation and prayer, and sharing. Sikhism emphasizes mastering five negative forces: Lust, Anger, Worldly or Materialistic Attachment, Conceit, and Greed. These together constitute what Sikhs term Haumai—"I am-ness." Mastering Haumai is achieved by developing five positive forces: Compassion, Humility, Contemplation, Contentment, and Service (seva) without expecting any material or spiritual reward. The guiding principles are Love and Forgiveness. Every decision in life has to be based on Rationality and a personal code of ethics. Guru Nanak's philosophy of values inspires the individual to transcend his/her existence through this spiritual discipline. Sikh religion preaches strong family involvement. A person pursuing this spiritual discipline must also work to create an atmosphere for other members of the family to progress spiritually.

The ideal Sikh has an intense desire to do good

The third postulate is that the true end of human beings is in their emergence as God-conscious beings, who remain aware of the earth and operate in the mundane material world, with the object of transforming and spiritualizing it into a higher plane of existence. In this spiritual state individuals are motivated by an intense desire to do good, transforming their surroundings.

Through a life based on the method prescribed by the Gurus, humans may achieve a higher spiritual state. Such truly emancipated, valiant, and enlightened spirits (jivan-mukta, brahma-gyani) become the true benefactors of humanity and the world around them. Such an individual would not exploit another human or sentient being, as each is a manifestation of the eternal and the supreme. In this God-conscious state they see God in all and everything.

> I perceive Thy form in all life and light;
> I perceive Thy power in all spheres and sight. (464)

Spiritualization is a liberation from material compulsions and attractions. It means an awareness of the Cosmic Order and striving toward the execution of Divine Will. So, the spiritualized human is creative and constructive. Therefore, a Sikh life is a life of harmony with other individuals, with other beings, and with other forms. For an enlightened individual the world has only one purpose: to practice spirituality. That is the ultimate objective of all humans.

Such a person is involved in human problems and society and has to prove his or her effectiveness there. Such a person lives with a mission—and works for the emancipation of all. A true Sikh is for individual human rights, the environment, and justice for all.

> The God-conscious person is animated with an intense desire to do good in this world. (273)

Practicing the philosophy

Integrated approach: Care of the environment without social justice is not possible

Environmental concerns may be viewed as part of the broader issue of human development and social justice. Many environmental problems, particularly the exploitation of environmental resources in developing nations, are due to the poverty of large parts of the population. Therefore an integrated approach is necessary.

Sikhism opposes the idea that the struggle of the human race is against nature and that human supremacy lies in the notion of "harnessing" nature. The objective is harmony with the eternal—God—which implies a life of harmony with all existence. Striving for a life of harmony, therefore, also implies a life of supporting individual rights and environmentalism—a life that works against injustice toward anybody and anything.

The tenth Guru in 1699 founded the Order of the Khalsa, whose members practice the spiritual discipline of Sikhism and are committed to ensure the preservation and prevalence of a World Society. Over the last three centuries the members of the Khalsa order have stood up for the rights of the oppressed and the disenfranchised even at the cost of their own lives. The Khalsa vision of the World Society is:

Henceforth such is the Will of God:
No man shall coerce another;
No person shall exploit another.
Each individual has the inalienable birthright
to seek and pursue happiness and self-fulfillment.
Love and persuasion is the only law of social coherence. (74)

The Khalsa have opposed any force that has threatened the freedom and dignity of human beings. In the eighteenth century it was the oppressive rulers of northern India and invaders from Afghanistan; in the nineteenth and twentieth centuries they have struggled against oppression by European colonists and Indian governments. For the Khalsa, justice requires the participation and inclusion of all in obtaining and enjoying the fruits of God's creation. Justice achieved through cooperative effort is desirable. The ideal for the Khalsa is to strive for justice for all, not merely for themselves.

The institutions of sangat, pangat, and langar

The Sikh Gurus, through their lives, provided role models for the Sikhs. They all actively worked to stress the equality of all humans and challenged the rigid social stratification of the caste system in India. The very existence of the Sikh religion is based on challenging:

1. Inequality in society, and
2. The exploitation of the poor and the marginal by the religious and political establishment.

Sikh Gurus provided many examples of standing by their principles and confronting exploitation and oppression. They stood by the "low" and the "poor," for, as Guru Nanak said:

There are the lowest men among the low castes.
Nanak, I shall go with them. What have I got to do with the great?
God's eye of mercy falls on those who take care of the lowly. (15)

Sikh Gurus challenged the status quo and came into conflict with the entrenched elite—political, social, religious, and economic. The Gurus were most sympathetic to the downtrodden of society, the untouchables and those of lower caste. They vehemently opposed the division of society on the basis of caste, which had been and is still significantly present. They identified themselves with the poor in full measure and were critical of those responsible for their misery. In the course of their travels they preferred to live in the homes of those who made an honest living rather than in the homes of the rich who thrived on exploitation.

Two Sikh Gurus were martyred by the regimes of their period for challenging the contemporary authorities. One of them, Guru Tegh Bahadur, was martyred when he stood up for the religious freedom of the Hindu inhabitants of Kashmir who were being forced to accept Islam by the rulers.

Sikh Gurus also molded traditional lifestyles to exemplify a more equitable society. They created many institutions that form the basis of Sikh society and are based on the equality of all. The Sikh Gurus invited people of all castes and creeds to meditate together. That would be called sangat. Either before or after the meditation, people were asked to sit and eat together irrespective of their social background, to create a sense of equality. That process would be called pangat. Sikh Gurus started a tradition of free distribution of food to the rich or poor through the Sikh meeting areas. That would be called langar. These three ideas were in contrast to the practices of Indian society, which had separate temples or water wells for social outcasts. These changes by the Sikh Gurus created a lot of opposition from the religious establishment, but they remain much alive in Sikh practices today. Through the creation of the Khalsa, the Gurus established a system that would protect and maintain a free and just order.

Equality of women

Women and their rights have been ignored for too long. Any approach to solving problems of social justice and the environment must be sensitive to women's concerns and must include women as equals.

Often piecemeal solutions to environmental problems focus on limiting population growth and on family planning programs. Most family planning measures end up abusing women's rights and should be rejected on those grounds alone. Meanwhile they spread mistrust of family planning among women.

Guru Nanak and other Sikh Gurus during their lives advocated equality and dignity of women and took steps to implement these principles. Guru Nanak denounced the idea that spirituality was only for men, and not for women. The first Sikh Guru in his preaching and writings made direct statements emphasizing that women were no less than men:

> After the death of one's wife, one seeks another,
> and through her social bonds are cemented.
> Why should we condemn women who give birth to leaders and rulers?
> Everyone is born of a woman and a woman alone.
> Nobody is born otherwise.
> God alone is an exception to this rule. (473)

Guru Amar Das strongly opposed the custom of sati in the sixteenth century and also advocated widow marriages. Sati was the Indian practice whereby a widow burned herself with her husband's corpse at cremation. Guru Amar Das appointed and ordained a large number of women preachers, and at least one female bishop, Mathura Devi, 400 years ago. The Sikh Gurus also raised their voice against the purdah or veil. Guru Amar Das did not even allow the Queen of Haripur to come into the religious assembly wearing a veil.

The immediate effect of these reforms was that women gained an equal status with men. Those who lived as groveling slaves of society became fired with a new hope and courage to lift themselves to be equals of the best in humanity. The spirit of the Sikh woman was raised with the belief that she was not a helpless creature but a responsible being endowed with a will of her own, with which she could do much to mold the destiny of society.

Women came forward as the defenders of their honor and dignity. They also became the rocks that stood against tyrants. Without the burden of unnecessary and unreasonable customs, Sikh women became the temporal and spiritual supporters of men, often acting as the "conscience of men." Sikh women proved themselves the equals of men in service, devotion, sacrifice, and bravery.

Since the late nineteenth century, Sikh community organizations have made efforts to expand educational opportunities for all. Individual Sikhs, men and women, in various cities and towns took the initiative to start and operate women's colleges and schools. Women's education was part of the drive to improve education among the Sikhs, initiated by Sikh organizations in the 1920s. In towns and villages in the Punjab, and in cities with significant Sikh populations, there exist schools and colleges operated by Sikh organizations.

Community-based sharing of resources

Traditional modes of farming and traditional modes of life in northern India have been dependent upon limited resources. As there exist circumstances where large numbers of people depend upon relatively scarce resources, the traditional lifestyle ensures use of the least resources, considerable reuse, and recycling. In a culture based on organic materials, recycling is an intrinsic and natural part of the resource cycle. There are strong traditions of sharing.

There have been traditional practices that maintained lands and forests as community property within proximity of human habitation. For instance, in traditional rural India and Punjab, two of the most important centers of human activity have been the Sikh gurudwara and a source of water—pond, tank, pool, or running water. Both of these sites were surrounded by community land, not owned by anyone and not used for agriculture. This was where there were trees and plants, such as groves or small forests. They provided shade and shelter, and were a source of firewood within easy reach of habitation.

The Gurus established towns and cities, each created around a religious center. The focus was on a lifestyle based on sharing: a lifestyle that promoted equity among people and optimum utilization of resources. Even today, rural Punjab families share resources with their neighbors. This is particularly evident on large family occasions such as weddings, when the entire village may play host to guests and share living space, beds, and so on.

Most gurudwaras in India were specifically designed to have a water tank or were near running water (rivers or pools), which were always considered a community resource. For instance, Amritsar grew up around the Harimandir (ordinarily referred to as the Golden Temple) and the Amrit Sarovar (the pool of nectar, that is, the water). The cities and towns that grew around gurudwaras were ideally centered on a spiritual lifestyle based on sharing.

Since the time of the Gurus, Sikh gurudwaras have included institutionalized practices that emphasize sharing of resources. Gurudwaras, in addition to being places where people congregate for prayer and meditation, are a place to stay for travelers and others; a community kitchen (Langar); a place for dispensing medication and medical care; and a place to impart education to the young. Gurudwaras have always been places of shelter for travelers and visitors, and most major gurudwaras have rooms where visitors may stay. In addition, Sikh gurudwaras stock extra beds, sheets, pots and pans, etc. At weddings and other family events, the gurudwaras are a source for borrowing these items.

There has always been great emphasis on avoiding waste. Traditionally the community kitchen served food on plates made from leaves and cups made from clay. Today they tend to use steel plates and utensils that are reused. The kitchens have always been stocked by ordinary people—farmers, traders, others in the community—on a voluntary basis.

Sikhism against smoking

It is now a known fact that smoking is both a primary and secondary health hazard. In addition to harming the environment, it has seriously deleterious effects on the person who smokes, on the bystander who breathes the secondhand smoke, and on the unborn fetus of the female smoker. Though this has been scientifically verified only in the last half century, Guru Gobind Singh, the last living Guru of the Sikhs, listed the use of tobacco as one of the four major acts forbidden to initiated adherents of the Sikh religion. Though tobacco was introduced into India only in the mid-1600s, he had the wisdom to specifically interdict it in 1699. From its very beginning, Sikhism had forbidden the use of any intoxicants or mind-altering substances for any purpose, except medicinal.

Conclusion

The ideal for Sikhism is a society based upon mutual respect and cooperation and providing an optimal atmosphere for individuals to grow spiritually. Sikhism regards a cooperative society as the only truly religious society, as the Sikh view of life and society is grounded in the worth of every individual as a microcosm of God. Therefore, an individual must never be imposed upon, coerced, manipulated, or engineered:

> If thou wouldst seek God, demolish and distort not the heart of any individual. (1384)

All life is interconnected. A human body consists of many parts; every one of them has a distinct name, location, and function, and all of them are dependent upon each other. In the same way, all the constituents of this universe and this earth are dependent upon each other. Decisions in one country or continent cannot be ignored by others. Choices in one place have measurable consequences for the rest of the world. All are part of the same system.

Life, for its very existence and nurturing, depends upon a bounteous nature. A human being needs to derive sustenance from the earth and not deplete, exhaust, pollute, burn, or destroy it. Sikhs believe that an awareness of that sacred relationship between humans and the environment is necessary for the health of our planet and for our survival. A new "environmental ethic" dedicated to conservation and wise use of the resources provided by a bountiful nature can only arise from an honest understanding and dedicated application of our old, tried and true spiritual heritage.

Appendixes

All passages are from the Guru Granth Sahib.

1

Through countless ages
Complete darkness prevailed;
In a complete void
There was no world, no firmament.
The Will of the Lord alone existed
Neither night nor day, neither sun nor moon;
Only God in an endless trance.
Neither creation, nor destruction, neither coming nor going;
There were no continents, no underworlds;
No seven oceans, no rivers, no flowing waters;
There were no higher, middle or lower planes;
Neither was there heaven, nor hell;
Neither death nor time;
There was no world of tortures, nor region of bliss;
Neither birth nor death;
When He so willed, then He created the world,
and without any support sustained the firmament.
He founded the continents, solar systems, underworld,
and from the Absolute Self, he became manifest.
None knows his limit, It is through the True Teacher (Guru)
the secret is revealed. (1035)

2

The forms become in according to Divine Will.
Human comprehension fails at this stage to understand
    the Divine Will. (1)

3

Guru Nanak describes:
Hundreds of thousands of worlds beneath and over ours. (3)

4

True are Your Universes, and true are your solar systems,
True are Your Worlds and true Your Creation,
True are Your doings and all deliberations,
True is Your order and true Your courts. (438)

5

Let truth be the strict norm of all you think and do, so that your
 pain and anxiety may go and all-felicity come to you,
Always cognize the near presence of God, through the practice
 of the Name,
Avoid hurt or injury to any sentient being so that peace may come
 to your mind,
Be humble by helping and serving those afflicted with misery and
 want so as to achieve God-consciousness.
Nanak testifies that God is the exalter of the fallen and lowly. (322)

6

Hail the Guru, for he teaches the ascent of man over himself. (462)

7

All nights all days all dates all occasions
All seasons, months, the entire Earth and all its load.
All Waters all winds, all the fires and underworlds.
All spheres, all divisions of Earth, and all worlds, men and forms.
How great is the Lord's command over them all cannot be known
Nor can the Lord's deeds be described.

8

The air is deemed to be Guru, Water the father and the Earth our
 mother, Whose belly gives us all the things.
Night and day are the two female and male nurses.
Made to play thus, the world plays in their lap.
You Yourself are the fish and yourself the net.
You Yourself are the cow and the grazer
Your light pervades in all the beings of the world just as lord has
 willed. (1021)

9

One who realizes the visible as merged in the formless,
And finds poise in the truth of God's invisible power,
Such a one shall not be subject to the cycle of births. (414)

10

A godly person covets not any women except his legal wife.
His relations with other women are governed by profound respect.

17

Zoroastrianism

This statement was prepared by the Athravan Education Trust and Zoroastrian Studies, the two main academic bodies responsible to the Zoroastrian faith for theological developments and study.

> *Whoever teaches care for all these seven creations, does well and pleases the Bounteous Immortals;*
> *then his soul will never arrive at kinship with the Hostile Spirit.*
> *When he has cared for the creations, the care of these Bounteous Immortals is for him,*
> *and he must teach this to all mankind in the material world.*
> —Shayasht ne Shayast (15:6)[1]

These actions, according to Zoroastrianism, will lead toward "making the world wonderful," when the world will be restored to a perfect state. In this state the material world will never grow old, never die, never decay, will be ever living and ever increasing and master of its wish. The dead will rise, life and immortality will come, and the world will be restored to a perfect state in accordance with the Will of Ahura Mazda (Lord of Wisdom).

The role of humanity in the world is to serve and honor not just the Wise Lord but the Seven Bounteous Creations of the sky, water, earth, plants, animals, man, and fire—gifts of God on High to humanity on earth.

The great strength of the Zoroastrian faith is that it enjoins the caring of the physical world not merely to seek spiritual salvation, but because

---

1. The Shayasht ne Shayast is a compilation of miscellaneous laws dealing with proper and improper behavior.

human beings, as the purposeful creation of God, are seen as the natural motivators or overseers of the Seven Creations. As the only conscious creation, humanity has the ultimate task of caring for the universe.

The faith endorses the caring of Seven Creations, as part of a symbiotic relationship. Zoroastrianism sees the physical world as a natural matrix of Seven Creations in which life and growth are interdependent if harmony and perfection are to be the final goal.

This goal is to be achieved by recreating the primeval unity of a perfect world, unpolluted and unsullied, as was first conceived by Ahura Mazda, the Wise Lord. In helping to bring about a state of perfection in this world and in the Seven Creations, Zarathushtra enjoined his followers to tread an ethical and righteous path. This is to be accomplished by integrating in one's life the divine attributes imbued by Ahura Mazda in each of the Seven Creations. For Zoroastrians, it is essential to recognize the essence of wisdom (spirit of humanity) and through it assimilate the right knowledge (the good mind symbolically represented by the cow and in turn the animal kingdom) in order to promote truth, order, and righteousness (the personification of truth as fire). This in turn will help one to exercise proper sovereignty (the all-encompassing sky) over life, the world, and the universe. The proper exercise of sovereignty (best power) will create a just order, which in turn will result in extending devotion (spirit of the earth) to the Seven Creations, creating perfection (of the blessed waters) and making the world wonderful and immortal (spirit of plants) for all times to come.

This is only possible if one shows responsibility toward the Wise Lord's creations. Those who perpetrate pollution and cause the defilement of all that is natural and good in the world are antithetical to the creations and to the Wise Lord Himself, as the physical world is made for the benefit of all who exist and live in the world. They must keep the Wise Lord's world pure (pak) while living life to the fullest and participating in the goodness of the Seven Creations. Zarathushtra also recognized the existence of a fundamental dualism operating in the relative world which at present is subject to a cosmic struggle. The Bounteous Spirit, Spenta Mainyu, guardian of the sky, upheld the foremost principles of existence, and is seen as the life-giving force, bringing light and righteousness into the world. In antagonism to the Bounteous Spirit is the transient existence in the relative world of the agency of excess and deficiency, a malevolent, hostile Evil Spirit. This spirit is held to be a life-negating force, bringing disorder and death, for its innate nature is to seek to destroy the Good Creation of Ahura Mazda. The world is seen to be in eternal conflict that will eventually resolve in the triumph of Good over Evil at the end of the limited time, in fulfilment of a firm promise made by Ahura Mazda.

Humanity is commanded to play an active role in this struggle, to assist Ahura Mazda in annihilating evil from the world. This eventual triumph of Good is achieved through the constant use of the ethical principle of good thoughts, good words, and good deeds, the baseline from which all actions of a Zoroastrian must spring.

A further injunction imposes an even greater responsibility: the cumulative righteous actions of all humanity are vital as they strengthen the power of Ahura Mazda and diminish the power of the Evil Spirit, Ahriman. This power, energized through the implementation of good thoughts, good words, and good deeds, is necessary in the present world to combat evil. This continuous strengthening of Ahura Mazda is required in order to make God truly omnipotent at the end of limited time, when evil will be vanquished forever.

The Zoroastrian devotion to the creations is not only brought to the fore in the form of litanies of praise dedicated to the creations, but is inextricably woven into the ritual practice of the faith. The most frequently performed Zoroastrian ritual is the jashan ceremony, which is a thanksgiving ceremony reenacting the perfect moment of creation when all was harmony. It is interesting to note that in the elaborate layout of the ritual the demarcated area on which the ceremony is performed is seen as representing the sacred earth, and the other six creations of sky, water, plants, animals, humanity, and fire are symbolically represented on it. The ceremony propitiates the Seven Creations, making a Zoroastrian conscious of the responsibilities toward reestablishing the pristine order of the universe as created by Ahura Mazda. The Zoroastrian concern for regarding the earth as sacred extends beyond life into the practices relating to death as well. In Zoroastrian tradition, death is not seen as the work of God but as the temporary triumph of the Evil Spirit, and this unparalleled eschatological understanding has given rise to a unique system. The method used for disposal of the dead body reflects this religious view. The corpse, seen as being afflicted by Evil and therefore polluted, is neither interred nor burned nor cast in the sea, but is exposed to the elements and birds of prey in a roofless stone tower. Thus, there is little despoiling of the elements.

The Zoroastrian Prophet Spitaman Zarathushtra (Greek Zoroaster) lived and preached in the great Iranian homelands, northeast of the Aral Sea. The Prophet in his divinely inspired hymns, the Gathas, spoke of a perfect world created by One Supreme, Eternal God, whom he recognized as Ahura Mazda, the Lord of Wisdom. He perceived Ahura Mazda in his primordial preeminence to be Wholly Wise, Good, and Just. Zarathushtra saw God to be perfect and ethically excellent.

In Zoroastrianism, Ahura Mazda is seen as the first cause of all things Good in the universe. The universe in turn is set in accord with the concept of Asha, an ordered Truth, governed by Righteousness. In the Gathas, Zarathushtra's sacred hymns, Ahura Mazda is seen as the Father of Asha, who has established the course of the sun, moon, and stars and upheld the earth and heavens. It is He who sustains the waters, the plants, the winds, and the clouds. He is the Creator of Light, Life, and Righteousness. Aiding Ahura Mazda in ensuring the welfare of the universe is the guardian spirit of man, the Fravashi. It is with the splendor and glory of the Fravashis that Ahura Mazda is said to have set in order the physical world, and it is through them that the world is kept in motion.

As part of the message of revelation, Zarathushtra defines in the Gathas the best existence for all humanity. "This man, the holy one, through righteousness, holds in his spirit the force which heals existence and is beneficent unto all as a sworn friend is" (Y.44.2).

Moreover, there is assurance that fury will be suppressed, violence put down, and righteousness ensured by rewarding the Good Mind (Y.48.7). His followers are promised that a future Savior will be sent to redeem the world torn by strife. Ahura Mazda's world was created with an ordered moral purpose of ultimately engineering the defeat of the Evil Spirit, and humanity functions to ensure the best existence by removing all that is evil.

The Zorastrian Story of Creation recounts the malicious assaults of destruction by the Hostile Spirit. The sky is ravaged and rent apart; the waters and earth are despoiled; the primordial plant withers; the good cow along with humanity is afflicted by disease and vices of all kinds; and into fire, the seventh creation, is mingled darkness and smoke.

The primeval despoiling of the world created with a good purpose mirrors society's role today, and this is what Zoroastrianism seeks to reverse. The religion uniquely attributes all that brings misery, hatred, vice, and pollution not to the whimsical acts of a Divine Being but to the unthinking attack of a malicious and hostile spirit whose innate nature is to destroy. As God's finest creation, we must strive toward a perfect world by combating the forces of Evil through a process of restoration and renovation.

Glossary

Advent: Period of 40 days prior to Christmas during which time Christians prepare for the celebration of the birth of Christ and his Second Coming.

Ashwin: The month in the Hindu calendar (October/November) at the end of which falls the festival of Divali.

Avalokitesvara: The One who Hears the Cries of the World. This Indian title was given to the notion of the compassionate Bodhisattva who, hearing the cries of the world, does not seek his or her own release but strives to save all suffering life. Avalokitesvara is the most popular deity in Mongolia and is known as Guanyin and Kwannon in Chinese and Japanese Buddhism, respectively.

Black Death: Plague that swept through Central Asia and the Middle East and into Europe during the late 1340s and killed an estimated one-third of the population.

Bodhisattva: In Buddhism, an enlightened soul who could cease existing, but who decides to continue in order to use the store of merit gained by many virtuous lives, to help suffering creation escape the terrible cycle of birth, death, and rebirth.

Bronze Age: Period of human history when stone tools were replaced by bronze tools, roughly 2000–500 B.C.

Canterbury: Famous pilgrimage site in England, renowned as the seat of the head of the English Church, the Archbishop of Canterbury, and as the site of the martyrdom of St. Thomas à Becket, murdered in the twelfth century for resisting the power of the king. It became the most popular pilgrimage site in Britain during the Middle Ages.

Christmas: Christian festival on December 25 celebrating the birth of Jesus Christ.

Counter-Reformation: Intellectual reaction to the challenge posed to Catholicism by the rise of the Reformation in the early sixteenth century. It led to a major overhaul of Catholic practice and theology in the mid-sixteenth century and established the form of the Catholic Church until modern times.

Dao De Jing: Chinese philosophical text written down around 500 B.C. and used as the basic text of Daoism. It is best translated as "The Way and Its Virtue."

Day of Judgment: A belief in Judaism, Christianity, and Islam that the world will end one day and that on that day, all who have lived will be judged and rewarded or punished according to their actions in this life.

Divali: Hindu festival of New Year, which comes at the end of the month of Ashwin.

Druze: Tradition that emerged in the eleventh century, combining elements of Judaism, Islam, and Christianity. It is a secret tradition and little is known of its teachings. Followers of the Druze religion live in Lebanon and Israel.

Easter: Christian springtime festival celebrating the resurrection of Jesus Christ from the dead. The name Easter comes from the pre-Christian goddess of spring Eostre.

Ecumenical: Promoting or seeking worldwide Christian unity, from the Greek word meaning the whole inhabited world. It has been used for the last 100 years to describe attempts by the Christian Churches to reunite or to work more closely together, trying to end centuries of disputes and tension between the different traditions.

Eid Ul Fitz: Muslim festival at the end of the fasting month of Ramadan.

Franciscans: The orders of monks and nuns founded by St. Francis in the twelfth century and one of the largest such Catholic orders in the world.

Guanyin: Chinese name for the Bodhisattva Avalokitesvara and the most popular deity in China.

Hajj: Annual pilgrimage to the Islamic holy city of Makkah in Saudi Arabia, which is one of the five requirements for Muslims. All Muslims are expected to go once during their lifetime if they can.

Icon: In Orthodox Christianity, a painted depiction of either Christ or the saints executed on wood and hung in churches or homes as an object of devotion.

Interfaith: Bringing together more than one religion, as for example in meetings, projects, or events.

Judeo-Christian: Arising from the biblical traditions of Judaism and Christianity.

Krishna: A major deity within Hinduism and traditionally seen as one of 10 incarnations (avatars) of the deity Vishnu, who is one of the three key deities of Hinduism. Krishna is the object of devotional tradition within Hinduism and many stories and legends surround him.

Lent: Christian period of fasting for 40 days prior to the festival of Easter.

Makkah: Holy city of Islam in Saudi Arabia, toward which all Muslims turn in prayer five times a day and to which they go on pilgrimage (the Hajj).

Mammon: Derogatory term used to describe the material or nonspiritual world.

Maronite: The main Church of Lebanon, founded in the sixth century A.D. by St. Maron. It follows Orthodox Christian traditions but is in full communion with the pope and the Catholic Church.

Messiah: The Anointed One of God, who in Jewish tradition will come to herald the Day of Judgment and in Christian tradition is Christ who will return at the End of Time.

Ordination: Confers the status of priest, monk, or nun in various traditions. In Buddhism, trees are sometimes "ordained" to give them the authority, status, and protection of being a monk.

Orthodox Christianity: The second largest tradition within Christianity after Catholicism. The Orthodox Churches are found from Eastern Europe through the former Soviet Union and are also strong in the Middle East. There are approximately 400 million Orthodox, and the Ecumenical Patriarch of Constantinople is the First Among Equals among the patriarchs of the various national Churches, such as those in Russia or Romania. The Orthodox do not have full communion with the Catholics because of theological differences.

Pagoda: Buddhist temple in countries such as Cambodia.

Pansa: Buddhist period of three months of fasting and retreat during the rainy season.

Pilgrimage: Tradition found in all faiths of going to a special site, often involving journeys lasting weeks and covering great distances. The actual act of going on pilgrimage is seen as spiritually beneficial in and of itself.

Pope: Head of the worldwide Catholic Church.

Prophet: In Judaism, Christianity, Islam, and the Baha'i faith, a person sent by God to reveal a proper relationship with God through his life, teachings, or transmission of the Word of God in the form of holy scripture.

Puja: Daily ritual at home and in temples involving worship and offering of food and drink to the deities, as performed in Hinduism and Jainism.

Qur'an: The Holy Book of Islam, revealed to the Prophet Muhammad in the early seventh century A.D.

Rabbi: Religious teacher within Judaism, usually associated with a local synagogue.

Ramadan: Islamic month of fasting prior to the festival of Eid Ul Fitz.

Reformation: Movement within Christianity that broke the Catholic Church apart in the early to mid-sixteenth century. From this movement emerged the Protestant Churches of northern Europe—Anglican, Lutheran, and Calvinist—which arose in protest against the corruption of the Catholic Church.

Rosh Hashanah: Jewish time of reflection and repentance prior to the festival of Yom Kippur.

Saint Francis: Catholic patron saint of ecology, who lived in the late twelfth and early thirteen centuries and is renowned for his teachings about care of nature. He founded the Franciscan Order.

Santiago de Compostela: Holy city in Spain where the body of the disciple of Christ, St. James, is believed to be buried. A major center for a thousand years of Christian pilgrimage and still immensely popular today.

Shamanic: One of the earliest religious traditions of humanity. Shamanism believes in two separate worlds—spiritual and material—between which only the shaman in a state of trance can travel to communicate.

Shariah: Islamic laws founded upon the Qur'an and on the development of precedent from the life of the Prophet Muhammad and other great figures of Islam.

Sutras: Buddhist and Hindu sacred books.

3iG: The International Interfaith Investment Group, established by ARC to enable the faiths to manage their investments according to socially responsible guidelines.

Vedic: A term used to describe the faiths in India, Hinduism and Jainism, that have their origins in the ancient books known as the Vedas.

Virgin Mary: The Mother of Christ, revered in Christianity and Islam.

Wesak: Major Buddhist festival associated with the birth, enlightenment, and death of the Buddha.

Yom Kippur: Jewish festival of New Year.

Selected Bibliography

Books and Articles

Berry, R. J. 1984. *God and Evolution: Creation, Evolution and the Bible.* London: Hodder and Stoughton.

Bowler, P. J. 1992. *The Fontana History of the Environmental Sciences.* London: Fontana.

Breuilly, E., and M. Palmer. 1988. *Christianity and Ecology.* London: Cassell.

Coleman, S., and J. Eisner. 1995. *Pilgrimage Past and Present in the World Religions.* London: British Museum.

Cooper, D. E. P., and A. Joy. 1992. *The Environment in Question: Ethics and Global Issues.* London: Routledge.

Crook, J. O. 1994. *Himalayan Buddhist Villages.* Delhi: Motilal Banrsidass.

Deane-Drummond, C. 1996. *A Handbook in Theology and Ecology.* London: SCM.

———. 1997. *Theology and Biotechnology: Implications for a New Science.* London: Geoffrey Chapman.

De Waal, E. 1991. *A World Made Whole: Rediscovering the Celtic Tradition.* London: Fount.

Dowley, D. T. 1990. *The History of Christianity.* Oxford: Lion.

Edwards, J., and M. Palmer. 1997. *Holy Ground: The Guide to Faith and Ecology.* London: Pilkington Press.

Gardner, G. 2002. "Engaging Religion in the Quest for a Sustainable World." Chap. 8 of *State of the World 2003.* Washington, D.C.: Worldwatch Institute.

Gosling, D. L. 2001. *Religion and Ecology in India and South East Asia.* London: Routledge.

Gottlieb, R. S. 1996. *This Sacred Earth: Religion, Nature, Environment.* New York: Routledge.

Hamilton, L. S. 1993. *Ethics, Religion and Biodiversity.* Cambridge: White Horse.

Khalid, F., and J. O'Brien. 1988. *Islam and Ecology.* London: Cassell.

Nasr, S. H. 1996. *Religion and the Order of Nature.* New York: Oxford University Press.

Oelschlaeger, M. 1994. *Caring for Creation: An Ecumenical Approach to the Environmental Crisis.* New Haven: Yale University Press.

Palmer, M. 1988. *Lord of Creation.* Godalming, U.K.: WWF-UK.

153

Palmer, M., and N. Palmer. 1997. *Sacred Britain: A Guide to the Sacred Sites and Pilgrim Routes of England, Scotland and Wales*. London: Piatkus.

Palmer, M., S. Nash, and I. Hattingh, eds. 1987. *Faith and Nature*. London: Rider.

Prime, R. 1988. *Hinduism and Ecology*. London: Cassell.

Triolo, P., M. Palmer, and S. Waygood. 2000. *A Capital Solution*. London: Pilkington Press.

Shiva, V. 1992. "Recovering the Real Meaning of Sustainability." In D. E. Cooper and J. Palmer, eds., *The Environment in Question: Ethics and Global Issues*. London: Routledge.

Smith, J. R. 2000. *Living with Sacred Space*. London: Shell Better Britain Campaign.

Tucker, M. E., ed. 1998–2003. *Religions of the World and Ecology*. 6 vols. Cambridge: Harvard University Press.

World Wide Fund for Nature. 1987. *Creation Harvest Liturgy*. Godalming, U.K.: WWF-UK.

———. 1988. *Advent and Ecology*. Godalming, U.K.: WWF-UK.

Websites

Baha'i Faith

Baha'i International Community. Official website of the Baha'i faith.
www.bahai.org

Buddhism

Khmer-Buddhist Educational Assistance Project. Founded in 1988 to help Cambodian temple communities on development programs.
www.keap-net.org

Mlup Baitong. A Cambodian NGO working to increase conservation through education, training, and advocacy.
www.mlup.org

Tibet Environmental Network in Ladakh, India.
www.aptibet.org/ten.htm

Christianity

A Rocha: Christians in Conservation. A Christian network preserving wetlands and other important areas in Portugal, Lebanon, the United Kingdom, and elsewhere.
www.arocha.org

Evangelical Environmental Network.
www.creationcare.org

Earth Ministry. A Christian ecumenical, environmental, nonprofit organization based in Seattle.
www.earthministry.org

EcoCongregation. Network for "green" churches in Great Britain and Ireland.
www.encams.org/ecocongregation

National Council of Churches of Christ in the U.S.A.
www.ncccusa.org

Web of Creation. Interfaith organization providing online environmental resources for faith-based communities.
www.webofcreation.org

Hinduism

Declaration on Nature: The Hindu Viewpoint. From a personal website (Dr. Karan Singh).
http://www.karansingh.com/environ/dec01.htm

Friends of Vrindavan. A U.K.-based community that aims to preserve and enhance the sacred forests and ecology of the Vrindavan region, based on the spiritual values of Hinduism.
www.fov.org.uk

Islam

Islam Science, Environment, and Technology. Islamic Medical Centre's environment index.
http://www.islamset.com/env/index.html

Harvard Forum on Islam and Ecology.
http://www.hds.harvard.edu/cswr/ecology/islam.htm

Jainism

Jain Study Circle.
www.jainstudy.org

Judaism

Noah Project: Jewish Education, Celebration, and Action for the Earth. A U.K. group raising environmental awareness in the Jewish community through education, festivals, and practical action.
www.noahproject.org.uk

Coalition on the Environment and Jewish Life.
www.coejl.org

Sikhism

Khalsa Environment Project. Sikh initiative "towards a greener world."
www.KhalsaEnvironmentProject.org

Zoroastrianism

UNESCO Parsi Zoroastrian Project.
www.unescoparzor.com

Zoroastrian College.
www.indiayellowpages.com/zoroastrian

Multifaith

Alliance of Religions and Conservation.
www.arcworld.org

Association for Forest Development and Conservation. An organization established to protect Lebanon's forests and to work toward achieving sustainable conservation of natural resources.
www.afdc.org.lb

Interreligious Coordinating Council in Israel. List of websites for environment and religion.
www.icci.co.il/linkpageecologyreligion.html

Harvard University Center for the Study of World Religions, Forum on Religion and Ecology.
www.hds.harvard.edu/cswr/ecology/index.htm

Interfaith Center on Corporate Responsibility.
www.iccr.org

National Religious Partnership for the Environment.
www.nrpe.org

About the Authors

Martin Palmer is secretary general of the Alliance of Religions and Conservation (ARC) and with HRH Prince Philip designed the original Assisi Event in 1986, which launched much of the work described in this book. An Anglican Christian, he studied theology and religious studies at Cambridge University. He has written many books on world religions and is a translator of classical Chinese sacred texts such as the Dao De Jing (Tao Te Ching) and Zhuang Zi (Chuang Tzu). He is a regular contributor to BBC radio on religious, ethical, and historical issues.

Victoria Finlay works as media advisor to ARC. She studied social anthropology at St. Andrew's University, Scotland, and William and Mary, Virginia, after which she joined Reuters. For five years she was arts editor of the *South China Morning Post* in Hong Kong. Her first book, *Colour: Travels through the Paintbox*, was published in 2002.

Index